Tiger: The Cat Who Thought He Was A Dog

Who Thought He Was

Meet the cat who was raised with dogs

Hannelore Clark

ISBN (Print): 978-1-09836-684-1
ISBN (eBook): 978-1-09836-685-8

This book is dedicated to my wonderful husband Dennis, who at first did not want to keep this orphan kitten, but later fought for every breath of Tiger's life, and that was more than once.

Dennis believed that anyone who did not love animals had no soul.

GINGER

Dogs and cats were always a big part of my life, and as a child I grew up with German Shepherds and different kinds of cats. Dogs also became a big part of my children's life, and mostly they grew up with two dogs and our cat, Tiger. The boys learned to treat the pets kindly and to be patient.

Nora, our beloved ten year old St. Bernard passed away suddenly, and Joey, our black Labrador Retriever was two months old when he came into our household. Seven-year-old Nora took to him like a mother to her pup. As for Joey, he adored Nora, following her around wherever she went and then cuddling up to her when she lay down to take a nap. Sometimes he would stand between her front legs and do his puppy bark – it was so cute! But mostly, Joey played with her for hours, pulling her tail or ears, and Nora took it all in stride. Their strong bond made them inseparable until Nora's passing.

Our family was devastated by the loss of our faithful Nora, but Joey fared even worse. Inside the house, he was depressed and stopped eating. He howled non-stop in our front yard, as if Nora might hear him and come home, even though he had been with Nora when she died on a Sunday morning.

By the following Friday, I couldn't face another day watching Joey's suffering and I decided he needed a companion to help him overcome his loss.

That Friday I picked up Michael from school at 3 p.m. and informed him that we needed to go to the city pound to inquire about adopting a rescue dog.

On our arrival, we were both overwhelmed by the incessant loud barking coming from the kennels.

The city pound was busy catching dogs that were roaming loose around the city. Then the dog's owner had to claim their dog and pay a stiff fine. Unfortunately, many dogs were never picked up, so the poor animal ended up being humanly euthanized, if it wasn't adopted by a new owner.

There were no dog licenses required in those years, and it was not uncommon for dogs to be on the loose. In which case, a dog catcher would be called to fetch the animal. Later, dog licenses became law, and a bylaw officer was hired to keep animals under control, including loose life-stock.

The dog pound was a gray brick building with chain-link wire fencing in the backyard of the complex, where some dogs were having fun running around and playing.

Upon our arrival, every dog charged to the fence to greet us with happy barking. Then once we were inside the building, the barking echoed so loudly that I could not understand what the officer was saying.

I had phoned him earlier to let him know that Michael and I were searching for a dog to be a playmate for Joey. So now there were eleven super friendly and cute dogs of different sizes and breeds greeting us from behind their kennel gate.

Except for one medium-size dog, who looked like a red fox and showed absolutely no interest in coming to the gate. Michael pointed to the dog and asked the man:" What about that dog?"

The man replied: "that's Ginger, I don't think you would want her because she is not well." Ginger was curled up into a corner against the wall, totally ignoring us.

I asked the man to let me into the small kennel to visit with her. I spoke softly and moved my hand over her back. When I reached her neck, she turned around and licked my hand ever so gently. Michael came in as well, and we both sat on the cement floor beside Ginger. She moved closer to Michael, and as he cuddled her, her tail started to wag.

I told Michael that she might be the one, and he agreed, smiling from ear to ear.

The officer came with her leash and suggested that Michael take Ginger outside for a little walk around the yard. I could see that the officer wanted to talk to me alone.

The story was: A family had brought Ginger to him because the father had been transferred to Vancouver by his company. The family was to live in a motel until they found a new home, and then they would come back and pick up Ginger. They paid for five months of boarding and also brought dog food. But five months came and went and there was no call from the family to inquire about Ginger's well-being.

The officer felt sorry for Ginger, and he would let her stay with him in his office whenever he was there. Ginger's food ran out after six months, and the man then fed her the dog-food that all the dogs in the kennel ate. However, Ginger was vomiting and had diarrhea. Obviously, she has been allergic to the new food.

He said he loved this gentle dog, who never barked or caused him any problems. He was not able to adopt her out, because the family had not signed a release paper for him to be able to do so. However, after six months she automatically became the city pound's property.

One Friday he decided to take her home for the weekend. He and his wife already had two big dogs that he brought home years earlier. His children were grown-up and had left home, so now it was just his wife and him living in the suburb on a big property. His wife loved Ginger, but she told him that it was another expense that she did not want to deal with. So, he brought Ginger back to the pound. In the meantime, she was in heat, and her health was deteriorating day by day. She was losing weight from all the vomiting.

We had arrived on a Friday, and that following Monday was the day when unwanted and sick dogs were to be humanely euthanized. Ginger's name was on that list! For me it was out of question for such a beautiful animal to be euthanized for no other reason than that she was in need of vet care.

I must have had tears in my eyes when Michael, very excited, rushed into the office looking at me anxiously. I told him not to worry, that we were taking Ginger home right away.

Happy Ginger followed Michael step by step into the car. A stinky dog in the car didn't matter to us. Her long fur was matted and dirty, but our professional groomer who always cared for Nora with love and gentleness would now treat Ginger the same way.

Michael and Ginger sat in the back seat, cuddling up like they were longtime bodies. Driving home was the easy part, but coming home was another matter.

Ginger was at the end of being in heat, but Joey, although neutered, still got overly excited and was ready to hump Ginger. Both dogs touched noses first, which was a good sign of instant acceptance, but I had to remove Joey immediately.

When we brought Ginger into the house and upstairs to the kitchen to introduce her to Dennis, he was appalled that we would bring such a scruffy dog into the house, never mind keeping her. Michael told him that Ginger is in heat and also vomiting.

"Dad, you always help the sick, and now we have to help this dog. She is mine now, and mom will not send her back to the kennel," he stated.

Dennis insisted that the sick dog be returned, but he lost the battle because Ginger was home to stay.

For the first three night, I kept her in the laundry room, made up a bed with lots of blankets, and left plenty of water to drink. On Monday morning, Dennis left very early for work. Michael took Ginger for a short walk around our property, while I cooked lean hamburger meat with rice for Ginger to eat in small portions. She didn't vomit, which was a plus. I also called the vet clinic, to take Ginger in that afternoon.

I told Dr. Thomas about Ginger's ordeal. She was still not groomed, and her nails were way to long.

The Doctor assured me that Ginger would be a beautiful gentle dog, and that she was extremely smart. He said he could tell by the way she let him touch her and handle her. He checked her teeth and figured that she was about three years old, still like a puppy. He also trimmed her nails.

His diagnosis regarding the vomiting was that Ginger most likely had a parasite from eating grass at the kennels. The vet gave her antibiotics and told me to bring her to the vet clinic in two weeks so she could be examined and spayed.

What a surprise it was for the staff of the vet clinic to see such a remarkable change in this dog two weeks later! Dr. Thomas complimented me, saying: "I knew you would do it – make a princess out of a tramp." He kissed Ginger's forehead, and she in return licked his face. We both had a good laugh.

During the day, Michael and I placed newspapers, and old blankets on the balcony off the second floor at the front of the house. No dog could harm her, and she had a roof over her head. We kept her in the laundry room at night and out of Dennis' site.

Dennis tried to convince me to buy another black lab puppy. I stood firm with a NO.

On Wednesday morning, Ginger was no longer in heat. She and I made another trip to town to visit the groomer. Theresa was shocked by Ginger's condition, and I said: "Just make her feel pretty." She warned me that she might have to shave all the dog's fur off.

What an improvement when we picked Ginger up after school! She was not shaved and her fur and tail were fluffy and shiny. What a beauty! Now she looked like a cute and smartly turned out a red fox. Theresa told me that she had partially cut the fur, and then groomed it carefully after giving Ginger a bath. She said that Ginger had really enjoyed being pampered and that she was an absolute pleasure to work with.

Michael and Ginger played in the back seat with a toy I had bought from the groomer's store. Ginger was an entirely different dog, clean and happy and beautiful.

At home, Dennis was speechless when he saw Ginger; he just kept shaking his head. After that, it didn't take long for Ginger to win Dennis' heart, once he realized how gentle she was and a delight to have around. My older son also took a liking to Ginger. So, she was now one of our family.

Joey and Ginger became happy companions, playing for hours and freely roaming throughout our property. They were each other's best friend.

After a while, our shy Ginger became very protective, guarding our house and yard. She growled and barked fearlessly if a car entered the yard. Not like Joey: he was friendly with everyone and probably would be even friendly with a burglar. We always knew when the BC Hydro employee had come to read the hydro meter at the back of our house because there would be numerous small blood stains on the white stucco of the house. Always excited about visitors, Joey would wag his tail so hard against the house wall that he would injure the end of his tail. So, he often walked around with a bandage on his tail.

A NEW PET IN THE HOUSE

On a Friday, mid-afternoon, it was a lovely autumn day in October 1979, and I looked forward to a relaxing weekend at our country home with my family. But before driving home I needed to buy dog food for our two dogs.

When I was buying dog food at the pet store, the last thing I expected was to come home with a kitten. Not just any kitten – this one was a newborn orange fluff-ball tabby. His eyes were still closed, but this little orphan sure got my attention.

In the store, along the right-hand wall, were fish-tanks of different sizes, and some had tiny tropical fish swimming in small tanks. Fish-tanks have heaters.

One small tank had no water and no fish. Instead, there was a tiny kitten swaddled in a tiny warm towel. The kitten was sound asleep.

The store clerk told me that a little 85-year-old lady had brought the six-day-old kitten to the store. Tiger, as she called him, was the only survivor of the litter of five kittens, when they were born.

Apparently, the mother cat was sitting in the driveway when a tenant drove into the yard at high speed and killed the cat instantly.

The woman was just beside herself, having lost both beloved felines at once.

But she knew that she could not take care of the tiny kitten, and she thought it would have a better chance to survive if she brought it to the pet store. Then someone younger would adopt the newborn kitten and take good care of it.

This is where I came in! It was a hasty decision and I made it without thinking; I instantly decided that I was prepared to take on the challenge of raising the orphan kitten.

When I brought little Tiger home to introduce him to my family, my husband was not pleased by the idea of a new kitten. Perhaps, I had acted too quickly by immediately bringing the needy little kitten home. I should have phoned my husband earlier to let him know of my plans.

We had been considering adopting a cat - an adult cat, that is - one that would take care of the enormous influx of mice that we experienced every fall. They would crawl into our basement so as to have a nice warm place in the winter. Dennis asked me to return the kitten to the pet store, and instead we would adopt two adult cats. But I refused to return little Tiger to the store because I had already fallen in love with my little kitten.

Caring for a newborn kitten totally changed our lifestyle. Life was never the same again, but I never regretted taking tender loving care of little Tiger. He flourished, and he became a very handsome tabby and a very colorful character. He was a social butterfly with our children and grandchildren, our close family members and our close friends.

Tiger, having been raised with two dogs, never met another cat until he was eight years old. He truly believed that he was one of the dogs, and he proved to be more protective of our surroundings and our house than the dogs were.

Every visitor, including friends, and also strange relatives who only came frequently to our house, had to deal with our cat. I had girlfriends calling me to tell me to hide Tiger away when they came for a visit, because they were afraid of him.

Tiger was difficult and ill-mannered when guarding our house – as he sat in his defense position on the seventh step of the stairway. No one could pass Tiger, or escape his growling and hissing, and lashing out his paws, until I came to tell him, that it was okay for the visitor to come upstairs. Then, having performed what he considered his duty, he would just walk away.

TIGER'S FEEDING
AND SCHEDULE

Taking care of a newborn kitten means playing with a little bundle of joy.

When I met this tiny newborn kitten, I felt instant connection, and all I wanted to do was care for and love this cuddly little orphan.

Once I had the kitten in my possession, all snuggled up in a small towel, I drove straight to the vet clinic.

Dr. Thomas checked the kitten's overall health and was pleased to find it in good condition. He then provided me with a lengthy consultation that was quite educational. He explained that young kittens have a high metabolism, and that with such a tiny stomach, they need feeding more often. That meant someone had to be around all day and night for feeding, until the kitten was old enough to eat solids. Also, the vet immediately switched Tiger's formula to a better brand from the U.S.

The Doctor handed me a small package of tiny bottles with nipples fit for a baby doll, and he gave me instructions. The bottles and nipples had to be sterilized for 5 minutes in boiling water. The powder formula was mixed with warm water, then stirred to create a milk-like liquid, and then drained into the tiny bottles. Dr. Thomas told me that the liquid had to be prepared fresh every two hours for four weeks.

For the first few days, the kitten drank 1 ml every 2 hours. Then each day I had to increase the amount by 0.5 ml per feed until it reached 10 ml per meal. Tiger was fed nine times daily!

Before handling Tiger, hand washing with sanitizing soap was important.

While being nursed, the kitten would lie on his back in the palm of my hand. Tiger took immediately to the bottle. Nowadays, one is advised to lay the kitten in a belly-down position, but I did as I was told 42 years ago. Then the kitten was weighed daily on my kitchen scale, to see if he was reaching the desired weight for his size and age.

At about seven days, the kitten's ear canals slowly began to open.

On the ninth day, Tiger opened his eyes for the first time, but his eyesight was still unfocused. He soon caught on that the bottle meant dinner and he would meow when he saw his bottle coming. He also learned to hold on to the bottle with his front paws while suckling. Kittens have no teeth until three weeks.

After about two weeks, he developed quickly, and he began to explore the world outside his basket. Ginger always kept a close eye on him.

It was just like having another baby in the house, except no diapers. After each feeding, the kitten had to be burped, just like a human baby. Basically, it took a lot of time to keep with the routine, but little Tiger was so adorable.

Mother cats stimulate her kitten by licking its genital area with her rough tongue, so that it will relief itself: then the mother immediately cleans up. But in this case, I was the mother. After each feeding, I covered Tiger's bottom with a Kleenex, then very gently rubbed his genital area with my index finger. Within minutes, he was urinating or having a bowel movement into the Kleenex. I then cleaned him with a moist soft cloth. It was just that easy.

At the age of four weeks, Tiger could walk and crawl around the house. He followed noise and he had good orientation. As Tiger became a Juvenile cat, he began to eat regular food; and at that point, I brought home a kitty litter tray and filled it with kitty litter. I placed Tiger in the tray, and as Mother Nature told him to scratch a hole so he could go to the bathroom, he did just that. My whole family was delighted; it was like having a toddler go potty for the first time.

For Tiger's bedding, I cut a soft baby blanket into small pieces and wrapped the kitten into a bag-like blanket. Then I laid him in a small basket and placed it near a warm heater.

Quite often, I would come to pick him up for feeding, and find that he was missing. I found out that Ginger would gently carry Tiger in her mouth to her bed, where he would immediately snuggle up to her chest and sleep. Tiger was the baby she never had, and Ginger turned out to be a devoted mother for our kitty.

When he was six weeks old, Tiger became quite active and very playful. He had good eyesight, and his eyes changed color from blue to yellow.

Because Tiger was born in the Fall, he was kept indoors until the cold winter was over and Spring finally arrived. How exciting was that? He was a constant source of amusement.

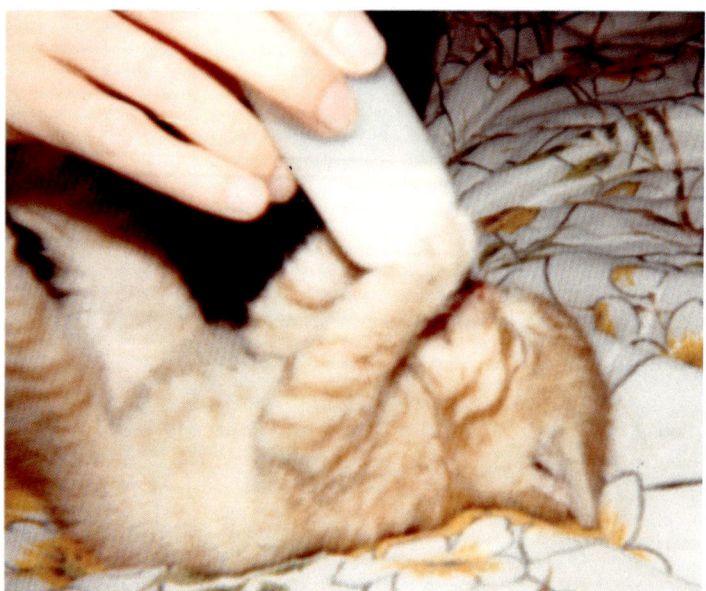

OUR TALENTED, ADORABLE ORANGE TABBY

During the winter, Tiger often sat on his perch in the big living room window and watched our two dogs playing in fresh powder snow in our backyard. Several times I would open the door so Tiger could check out, or at least smell the outside. But he was not impressed, and he would run right back up to his favorite spot in the window.

At six weeks of age, Tiger would walk 11 steps downstairs to the laundry room to use his litter box. He also learned to lap water from a dish and to eat solid food three times a day – which was half canned and half dry food. Vitamin B is essential for cats and it is mainly found in fish. Cats are carnivores so they need meat, and a balanced diet is important for the cat to stay healthy. Chocolate is toxic for cat and dogs, and so are some house plants so I removed most of my plants because I was not sure if they would be harmful to Tiger.

Just like people, cats can be lefties or righties. Researchers have watched cats reaching for food and they found that 40% were lefties. (I just thought you ought to know)

Cats meow for chatting, but they purr, hiss or shriek when they need to get their message across. They also use body language by rubbing against things with their tail and by spraying them; and they rub their faces on objects, or scratch on wood, to announce that they were there.

A cat's whiskers show their mood. For example, if they point forward, the cat is happy and feeling friendly; but if the whiskers are lying flat on the face, the cat may be aggressive.

Joey, our black Labrador retriever, tolerated Tiger, but if the kitten wanted to get his attention, Joey would just ignore him and walk away. But not our dog Ginger - she would let Tiger happily cuddle against her. She would lick the kitty until he closed his eyes and fell asleep, and then she would also go to sleep. So Tiger and Ginger became best friends. Also, the three-month-old kitten was smart, and he caught on to some tricks that would be rewarded with treats from his human admirers.

Our boys went through a lot of socks because they never wore slippers in the house, so I would take two worn socks and stuff them into another sock, and then put a knot on the outer sock. This made for a cheap, but greatly appreciated cat toy, and new ones were always available.

I would throw a stuffed sock down the staircase, and the dogs would shoot down to retrieve it and then bring it back up to me. Of course, they wanted me to repeat the game over and over again. Soon Tiger caught on to what the dogs were doing, and he would jump right into the game, so the dogs were now competing with Tiger. Our agile kitten would leap over the dogs and down the eleven stairs to reach the stuffed sock first and bring it back to me for another throw. We also used a soft ball that Tiger could hold on to. Joey the dog would soon give up the play, and then he would watch Ginger and Tiger as they retrieved the ball or sock. Tiger usually won.

Another pastime for Tiger was playing hide-and-seek by hopping into a large paper grocery bag. He would hide in there until Ginger started looking for him, and then he would jump out of the bag to attack her face. It was a game they played together during the cold winter months.

My boys gave up a few small stuffed animals for Tiger to play with, but the retrieving and paper bag games were his favorites.

There was also a problem with Tiger that was ongoing. It happened if we forgot to close one of the three bathroom doors before leaving home; and believe me, someone would always forget. Then when we came home, the toilet paper would greet us at the door entrance. Tiger was skilled at unrolling a new roll of toilet paper and tracking it through all the rooms in the house. And he would sometimes rip up the paper into thousands of pieces. Then after he was finished with his paper scattering, he would curl up in the sink and sleep.

When Spring arrived, Tiger was ready to venture outdoors, but before that happened, Tiger had to have all the necessary vaccinations.

He was also neutered once he weighed three pounds. Spaying and neutering cat or dogs makes a big difference, and it prevents over-population. Just one unaltered female cat and her offspring can produce 67,000 kittens in only six years! In seven years, one female cat and her offspring can produce an incredible 370,000 kittens.

TIGER'S HOUSE RULES

Tiger is not allowed on the chesterfield or on the furniture.

Now, Tiger can sleep on his little blanket on the chesterfield.

Besides sleeping in every sink; he also sleeps on every pillow in every bed of the house.

However, he is definitely not allowed on the kitchen counter.

Now, Tiger is on the kitchen counter, except if I prepare dinner.

Tiger does go wherever he wants and he does whatever he wants.

Tiger tried to wake me for his breakfast around 6:00 a.m., but then he had to wait because the dogs where to be fed first. Tiger's obedience went sideways. However, he had certainly trained me well.

I thought we adopted Tiger, but more likely, he adopted us.

REALLY, a Cat has NO Rules!

...I am thankful, that Tiger has never done any damage to our homes

MUSKRATS IN THE POND

May 1980 and as usual, our daily chores were yard work. At this time of year, the small pond came alive with run-off water from the ditches, where melted snow ran into the creek and then into the pond. Another creek ran out of the small pond, and into a large pond that was adjacent to our 15 acre lot.

There, beavers constructed their home by pilling up logs, sticks and shrubs to make a dam. With powerful jaws and strong teeth, they fell trees (mainly birch) in our backyard, and also in our neighbor's property that included part of the pond. The landscape began to appear as if it had been struck by a severe tornado.

Beavers' teeth continue to grow throughout their entire lifetime of 10 to 15 years!

Our pond was about eighty feet wide and slightly sloping downhill from the rockery garden. The water level had risen and there was lively movement in the water. Our little Tiger cat, always curious, walked slowly to the pond to see what the noise was all about and he sat at the water's edge to check things out.

Then suddenly Tiger let out a desperate cry, as he was struggling to stay on land. Immediately, our two dogs charged to Tiger's rescue, ferociously barking. Their rescue mission was successful, and the beast let go of my kitten. But the incident shocked my poor kitty and I had to hold him in my arms for over an hour to calm him down.

All I saw was a long brown furry animal aggressively trying to pull Tiger by his tail into the water. Obviously, it wanted to drown him. We had never seen a rodent before in the pond, and nor had I ever encountered muskrats anywhere else.

The next day, I watched a mama muskrat with three little offspring's swimming in the pond. Most likely she was trying to protect her kits from Tiger, who was by now nine months old. Even so, he was not strong enough or big enough to pose a danger to the muskrat family.

To me, the muskrat looked like a small beaver, except her skinny long tail pointed straight out of the water. This creature's normal habitat is wetlands, and their rat-like appearance, 50 cm in length and the size of a rabbit, is similar to that of water-rat rodents that are found all over the world.

Because muskrat carry disease, I had Tiger checked of by a vet. Fortunately, our cat had gotten away without a scratch, and for that I was grateful.

After that the muskrats were never seen again on our property. Most likely we just had too many children and dogs and visitors roaming the grounds.

GINGER TEACHING TIGER HOW TO CATCH A MOUSE

In the spring, as I raked the lawn to get rid of the winter debris and leaves, I noticed our dog Ginger carrying a big live field mouse in her mouth as she trotted down the driveway, and our big kitten Tiger was trotting along beside her.

Ginger dropped the mouse right in front of Tiger, but the rodent ran away. Nine months old Tiger did not realize that this was a lesson he was supposed to be learning: "How to catch a mouse."

Ginger jumped after the mouse to retrieve it, and again threw it in front of the kitten. But Tiger simply did not know what this was all about. He just stared at the fleeing mouse as if he was afraid to get near it, maybe he was afraid to be bitten.

The mouse escaped again, and Ginger grabbed the rodent once again and this time she crushed it with her teeth. Then she threw the dead mouse towards Tiger. This finally caught Tiger's attention, and he leaped towards the dead mouse, grabbed it with his front paws, and then threw it up in the air. This play he repeated for quite some time, until he lost interest and walked away.

For the next few weeks, Ginger again and again brought Tiger live mice for him to catch, but they were too big for him to handle. To him, playing with a dead mouse was much more fun.

Then in mid-June, much to my amazement, I observed Tiger in our field hunting for mice with Ginger. Ginger would still do the catching and then Tiger would run after the mouse. Then the dog would do the killing, as usual, and Tiger would play with the dead mouse.

Eventually, Tiger mastered the art of hunting on his own, but always with the faithful Ginger at his side.

Later, they ventured across the road to a 75-acre field of lush terrain, where the two buddies hunted for rodents. They always brought their catch home and proudly displayed the unfortunate mice at our front entrance. We Thanked them for the gift, and as usual, we had to be very careful not to step on a dead mouse in the dark.

With Ginger's persistent tutelage, Tiger proved to be a good hunter and he was always duly proud of his catch.

Relaxing after mouse hunt.

RUNNING WATER

Tiger's insatiable sense and curiosity included his desire to observe closely whenever a toilet was going through the process of being flushed.

When the toilet filled up with water, he could sit on the toilet seat and reach out to the water with his front paws, splashing and playing, and clearly having a lot of fun. Then when he was done with playing, he would have a drink of water from the toilet.

I would watch my cat's painstaking grooming ritual. Why would he go through all that trouble keeping himself clean and then drink from the toilet? Maybe toilet water tasted fresher and colder than stagnant standing water.

Our cat was also obsessed with the fountain of the bidet. He would cry and insist that it be turned on and filled with water. He would then play with the water and drink from the fountain. And he liked the water to be extra-cold.

He also liked the bathtub faucet to be left dripping so he could play under it, get his coat all wet, and then shake himself like a dog.

Then the water would be everywhere, and I would have to wipe off the walls and the floor.

There had to be a reason why Tiger slept in every bathroom sink of every house he ever lived in. Most likely it attracted him because it was a cooler place to rest, especially in the summer when the temperature started to climb. The shape of the sink accommodated Tiger's body quite well. If someone walked into the bathroom and the cat was sound asleep in the sink, he would just look up briefly, and then close his eye and resume his nap.

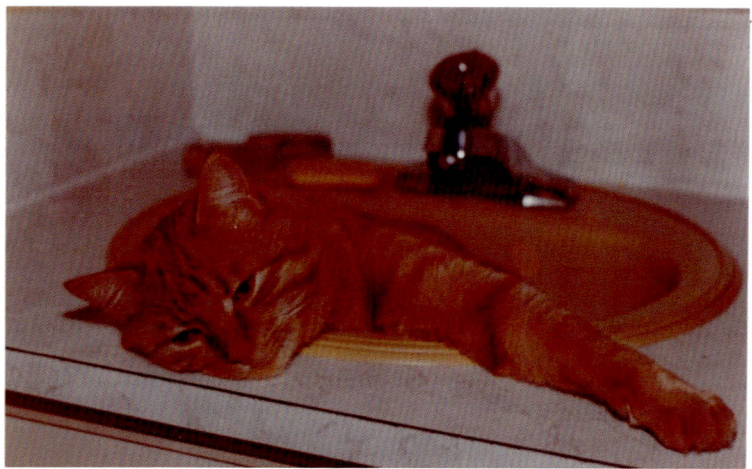

SPILLED COFFEE

Mornings, mostly during the week, were "me hours only." Dennis would leave the house for work and the boys were in school. That meant that Tiger and I had the house to ourselves while the dogs were roaming the yard. My routine was to relax with a mug of coffee and read a book or magazine, or phone friends, or families while sitting at the kitchen table. Tiger, who now weighed 24 lbs., was big enough to sit beside me on a kitchen chair.

One morning, just for the fun of it, I dipped my finger into the mug and let Tiger lick the coffee off my finger. Yummy, a taste of coffee with cream! It was more like a latte and it instantly became his favorite treat. After that, Tiger sat on his chair every morning, waiting for his spoon of special coffee to be served.

This was before cordless phones. In the 80's, we had a brick-size, mustard-color phone with a rotary dial and a long, curly cord attached to the kitchen wall. And we had a second phone in the master bedroom.

One day, the phone rang as I had just placed my fresh cup of coffee on the kitchen table. For some reason, I decided to answer the call in my bedroom and to relax on the bed while chatting with my German girlfriend.

I must have been gone for a while and I completely forgot about my coffee. I should have known better than leave Tiger in the kitchen by himself. Tiger must have been drinking from the cup before it tipped over, spilling the rest of the coffee on the table and the floor. When I walked into the kitchen, he was standing on his hind legs on my chair with his front paws on the table, eagerly licking the spilled coffee.

I was worried that such a large amount of coffee would harm my cat, but Tiger, once again, proved how tough he was. He showed no harmful-side-effects.

From then on, Tiger was served one tablespoon of coffee, instead of a small coffee spoon, every morning. This was our morning happy hour.

PLAYING WITH A GARTER SNAKE

Quite often, Tiger would drop off a special gift at the front entrance, and when we exited the house via front door, we had to be very careful not to step on dead mouse, or rat or bull frog. Tiger loved to pounce on moving things.

One day when I was working in the front yard, I saw our adventures cat dragging a dark gray serpent between his legs towards the front entrance. The snake's tail dangled from Tiger's mouth, and the head of the garter snake trailed behind on the gravel path. Tiger proudly released the snake on the front door mat.

The snake must have been scared out of its wits. Now cornered, it started thrashing wildly, in an attempt to escape, but the unfortunate serpent didn't have a chance. Tiger proceeded to play with it, making it curl up, and then Tiger would try to uncurl the snake with his front paws. So, it would curl up again only to be stretched out again.

This show went on for almost an hour, until the snake either became exhausted or pretended to be dead. At that point, Tiger lost all interest and walked away.

I picked up the snake and released it near the creek. Suddenly reviving, it slithered away and was gone within seconds.

THE JEWELRY THIEF

In winter, on weekend evenings, our family often settled in the living room to watch a movie on T.V. When Tiger suddenly sneaked by me dragging my gold necklace in his mouth. He would snatch any jewelry he could find laying on my bedroom dresser or on the bathroom counter. He then would hide his findings behind or in the bookshelf, and under the chesterfield or living room chairs. The heaters throughout our house had been a good hiding place for jewelry, but mostly it was hidden in the living room area, so as to be sure that we would find the stolen gems.

He preferred steeling rings. Most of my jewelry I brought with me when I immigrated from Germany to Canada. One particular garnet ring we could never find. It was special to me as it has been, a going- away gift from my grandmother. It belonged to a set that consisted of a garnet bracelet, necklace, earrings and brogue. We searched everywhere in the living room, but it was lost for good. It was my favorite ring.

One Christmas, my husband presented me with a beautiful maple-wood hand-crafted large jewelry box. But I would still leave a jewelry piece on my dresser, if I was too tired and forgot before going to sleep.

The day we moved out of the Beaverly home, Eve vacuumed the entire house. I asked Eve to look out for my garnet ring, and she found the garnet ring stuck between the fireplace stucco wall and the plush carpet. What a relieve it was for me to have my lovely garnet ring back!

It never failed when we entertained friends, that Tiger would walk into the living-room showing off his skills with a piece of jewelry. You could feel his pride as he circled around our feet. If I told him to drop it, before he had a chance to hide his stolen prize, he would let go of it at once and walk away.

One time, Tiger picked up Dennis' ring, but obviously it was too heavy for him to carry. He just threw it in the living-room and ran away.

Tiger only stole jewelry in his juvenile years; later, he got bored and searched for other adventures.

A NAKED ROBIN

When it comes to designing a rockery garden, first you need good soil and lots of it. Two dump truck loads were delivered to our yard, creating a long pile of dirt on the front lawn about the length of our house. I then covered the dirt with old carpets, bottom up (they had been removed from an old house and discarded). At that time landscaping fabric was unheard of, but the carpet did the trick and only a few weeds grew in the garden.

For three years we went rock hunting in the countryside – on mountains and in fast-running creeks, because you don't use just any kind of rocks; they have to be the right size and shape, and light in color. After spacing the rocks on the carpets, I then cut holes in the carpets between the stones and planted small flowering shrubs, hardy perennials, and colorful annuals, covering as much ground as possible.

Then there were the enhancements – a birdbath and blue heron and owl figurines made of cement - personal touches that made the garden seem more an intimate place. The retreat that I worked so hard to build looked fabulous as one drove into our driveway, and once completed, it required minimal maintenance.

One early Spring morning in 1982 as I worked on my rockery garden, I heard a frantic cry, like a bird in distress. To my horror, I saw Tiger in the driveway, about 100 feet from the house, dragging a medium-size bird between his front legs! The bird's feet were in Tiger's mouth, and the bird was on its back with his wings flat on the ground as it was dragged on the gravel by my cat. Immediately I threw a stone at Tiger, and when it hit him, he dropped the bird.

Tiger looked at me strangely and again picked up the bird, which was still lying on its back. Now as Tiger walked on, I panicked and threw another stone at Tiger, hitting his back. This time he yelped, and he dropped the bird and ran to the back of the house, leaving the bird lying on the ground.

I walked over to the bird – it was a robin – and I picked it up and checked for bite marks. To my relief, there were none. Either he had pretended to be dead or he was just totally traumatized. The robin did not make a sound as I held him in my hands, and he looked at me as though he was thanking me for his rescue.

I sat the bird down on a rock, and once he realized he was free, he flew up to the branch of a pine tree. Surprisingly, both of his wings were intact. However, once he was airborne, the poor robin lost most of his body feathers. So that summer we had a semi-naked Robin on our property.

By fall, all his feathers had grown back. He flew south for the winter with all his robin friends and returned the following spring.

Robins regularly return to the same breeding site each spring. Returning to the same location is a fairly common habit. They simply clean the old existing nest. Then they lay 2-5 eggs, which hatch within 20 days.

TIGER'S TERRIFYING
CAR RIDE

In February 1983, Dennis and I decided to escape the harsh winter for a two-week vacation in the south and enjoy the sun, sand and surf.

For Christmas we had purchased a new TV and a satellite dish, and the large white dish was now stationed in our front yard, attached to a tall stand.

While we were away, Eve took care of our household and stayed with my two teenage sons, Pete 17 and Michael 14. Eve, who lived just down the road from our house, had been working for me since 1970.

My son Pete worked part–time at McDonalds, and one Friday Pete told Eve that there was no need for her to stay that evening because he and Mike were staying home. Eve trusted the young men and went home, and Pete invited a few friends from work to our house to watch TV programs on our new Satellite TV. Our cat Tiger was also in the house. In the winter months, when he was kept indoors, his personality totally changed and he adopted a "don't mess with me" attitude. That evening he placed himself in the middle of the stairway that lead up from the front entrance to the living room where the TV was located.

When the teenagers came into our house, nasty Tiger stood his ground and would not let the visitor up the stairway, hissing and lashing out with his paw so they were not able to pass.

Pete did not tolerate the cat's behavior. He shoved him out the front door into the cold winter night, at a temperature of minus 20 degrees.

What was my teenage son thinking? Tiger's coat was not suitable for the cold, he was an indoor cat. To survive, he immediately had to seek shelter in a warm place and as we later found out, he did.

One of the girls visiting the house had a 10 p.m. curfew. She drove home in her dad's Ford 150 pickup, and she experienced trouble controlling the steering wheel on her eight km drive home. Once at home, she told her dad to have the steering fixed because she had almost driven off the road on highway16.

The next day at around 2:00 p.m., her dad started the truck and drove eight kilometers to the Husky Service Station on Victoria Street downtown. A mechanic opened the hood of the truck and there was our humble beast tangled up in the wiring of the motor! By some miracle, he had survived two terrifying car rides. And Tiger had, at that point, been tangled in that motor for over 18 hours!

He must have been extremely cold and scared, and he was clearly in pain from his terrific injuries.

When my husband and I arrived home, Pete and Michael had some explaining to do. Pete, ever so nervous, said that Tiger was not at home, but that he was okay. He then went on to tell us the story. I was furious and I told him that I would deal with him later.

Tiger was a big part of my life and our family's life. For me, the hurt was as if I had just lost a child.

Luckily, we had arrived home on a Sunday and I did not have to work on Monday. I called the SPCA, the City Pound, and the two veterinary clinics in town to try and locate Tiger. Our vet, Dr. Thomas, assured me that Tiger would most likely walk home. I placed a 'Lost' ad with Tiger's photo in the local Citizen Newspaper with the offer of a reward. Then several people phoned and offered me a new kitty.

Then a woman called to say that she had found Tiger. I doubted her story because of the location where she had apparently found my cat, and I drove there with mixed feelings. A little old lady met me at the gate and invited me into her house. The property looked like a junk yard, with old wrecked cars, fridges, oil barrels, etc. We walked a very narrow path to make it safely to her front door.

I was overwhelmed by the stench of cat urine, and the house was a filthy mess, overloaded with junk and empty alcohol bottles. Clearly the woman was a hoarder and a drinker. There were cats everywhere but all the felines seemed to be well fed, though definitely lacking veterinary care. Most of the cats had some type of mange or scabies, and many had pus in their eyes. In the corner, there were two females nursing kittens.

The old lady disappeared into another room and returned with a very healthy-looking orange tabby cat. Most likely she had picked him up off the street recently as his coat was shiny and healthy. He was clearly frightened and just wanted to escape her arms. I guessed that he was about a year old and weighted about 10 lbs. Tiger's weight was 24 pounds and he was about three times the size of this kitten.

My temper flared as I told her that this cat does not even know me. She explained that he might have some brain damage and therefore not remember me. She told me that the cat had been crying outside her door, and that she had let him in and immediately called me. Some people will do anything for a buck!

I told her to let the cat go home, and that there was no money to be made from trying to sell a stolen cat.

Furious as I was, after I arrived home, I phoned a friend who worked for Mental Health and Welfare. She got in touch with the right authorities to check out the situation, so that the woman and the cats could receive assistance.

For the next week, every evening after work Dennis and I walked through the back alley behind the Husky station frantically calling Tiger's name. We checked every corner and every opening, but there was no sign of any cat.

On day 13, I canceled the 'Lost' ad in the newspaper, hoping that Dr. Thomas was right – that Tiger would just appear at our door one day. Tiger has now been missing for 18 days.

Somehow, I had the feeling that I should have a face-to-face talk with the mechanic at the Husky station. The faithful Ginger, our female dog who had always been at Tiger's side, was about to be put to a test. She and I drove to the Husky station. The mechanic, a rough-looking man in his 30's, explained to me that he had cut the cat out of the wiring of the motor and Tiger had run off like a bullet. Laughing, he made the remark that once he had cut that darn cat loose, the mad feline bit into his fingers through his heavy leather work glove. He held a glove up to my face to show me Tiger's bite marks.

I felt relieved to know that my cat still had some fight in him and that he was a survivor.

Across from the Husky Station was the Slumber Lodge Motel, where I parked my car, put Ginger on a leash, and proceeded to walk around. Suddenly, Ginger sniffed at a side door of the motel, wagged her tail, and then sat down, refusing to go any further. I left her sitting there and walked into the office of the motel where I was greeted by a very friendly owner. I told him Tiger's story and showed him a picture.

Once he had seen the picture of my orange tabby and I offered him $ 50.00 for the return of my beloved cat. The man laughed and said: "Lady, for 50 bucks I would gladly give you your cat back, if I only had it." I left him Tiger's picture and wrote my phone number on the back. Ginger was still sitting beside that door. I tried to open it, but it was locked. Ginger refused to get back into the car, so I had to lift her in, and then we drove home. I was confused by Ginger's behavior and disappointed that we had not found Tiger.

The following day, when I was driving home from work, the phone rang. The owner of the motel said in an extremely loud voice: "Lady, where have you been all day? I have your cat!"

He had told his Portuguese chambermaid my story and let her know that if she found the cat, they would split the 50 dollars.

The chambermaid had replied:" I hear a kitten cry all the time up in that cupboard above the dryer. It sounds like a mama that has babies."

In fact, whenever Tiger had to ride in the car to the vet, he changed his voice and sounded like a crying kitten. It appeared that on the day Tiger was freed from the motor of the truck, he had jumped off the vehicle and ran towards the back alley to find the nearest safe place. He probably found a side door open and then disappeared into the building that turned out to be the Slumber Lodge.

It seems that he landed in the laundry room of the Slumber Lodge with its high commercial dryers, above which were cupboards containing supplies for the motel rooms. Then that afternoon when the chambermaid was re-stocking the rooms, she left the cupboard and the side door open for just a short time. Lucky for Tiger that he found that opening and jumped into the warm cupboard to hide. Then after her return to the room, the chambermaid closed the cupboard.

Once they opened the cupboard door with the two of them standing there, Tiger jumped out and ran towards the door, but it was closed. The man was prepared for Tiger trying to escape. It was a pet friendly motel, but with one exception – namely the pets had to stay in a kennel during the night. The motel offered kennels if the guests did not bring their own.

So, the motel owner had placed an open kennel on the laundry room floor, which was the next way out for Tiger. Realizing that the room door was locked, he ran straight into the kennel for another hiding place. The man closed the cage and then attached a water container. Apparently, Tiger drank three cups of water.

After the phone call, I drove immediately to the Slumber Lodge, and to my relief, there was my

Tiger! I lifted Tiger up, and to my shock I felt the wires sticking out of his chest and up to his shoulder, all with dried blood. Yet, he purred, licked my cheeks, and gave me a gentle love bite on my earlobe.

I have since learned that a cat purring can be pain related, and that purring may actually increase when the cat is experiencing pain.

Knowing that the veterinary clinic was closed for the day, I phoned from the motel office for the clinic's emergency number. To my surprise, Dr. Thomas was on call and he said he would wait for us at the clinic.

When we arrived, Dr. Thomas gave Tiger a checkup. He then gave him a sedative and wrapped him in a warm blanket. Once Tiger settled down, he dosed off. Then the doctor inserted an intravenous line for rapid administration of fluid, which was required due to the severity of Tiger's dehydration.

Dr. Thomas told me that injured felines live off their stool and urine while in hiding, so they can heal.

The following day, Tiger required major surgery to remove the wires from chest and left shoulder. He also had severe injuries and burn marks from the running motor and he ended up having 21 stitches, along with antibiotics to prevent infection. For the first few days, he had to be fed intravenously because he vomited when they tried to feed him soft can food. His stomach had been severely affected from not having food for 18 days.

Once Tiger was stable enough to eat small amounts of canned food on his own, he was able to return home. After Tiger spending 18 days in hiding, plus two weeks at the vet clinic, it was such a relief for all of us to finally hold Tiger in our arms.

Of course, Tiger had a long road to recovery, but at least he was home where he belonged. Ginger was overjoyed to have her buddy back. She did a happy bark and jumped like a baby lamb when Tiger's kennel was placed in front of her. Joey, on the other hand, just whacked his tail; his terror had come back home. Previously, Tiger had sometimes been nasty to Joey, and very bossy. Whenever Joey would come too close, Tiger would lash out at him. But this behavior completely stopped after Tiger's accident.

Now we had a new problem. Tiger was wearing a plastic collar to prevent him licking his wounds, which were healing nicely. Ginger had always a habit of licking the cat daily from head to toe, ever since Tiger was a kitten. Now we had to keep telling her not to do it, and she certainly did not understand why I was trying to keep her away from her darling.

So, the boys built a new perch for Tiger. They cut it out of a round drum and nailed it on top of a three-feet-high wooden pole. As for the base, Dennis used his table saw and cut a thick 30 by 30 inch piece of plywood. He then screwed the base at the bottom to the pole. Now the perch was stable. Then I covered the bed with baby blankets. We placed the new perch right by the window so Tiger could oversee the backyard. It was a perfect fit for him to rest and to sleep. He still needed to be lifted in and out of his new bed, but we could see that he was healing. As for Ginger, she was no longer able to reach him and lick him, so that problem was solved.

For weeks, Tiger slept most of the day, and his appetite slowly improved. Within 6 months he was himself again. And he learned his lesson – he had no desire to get anywhere near a car. Also, he became friendlier towards our close friends and family members. But he still did not accept everyone as a friend.

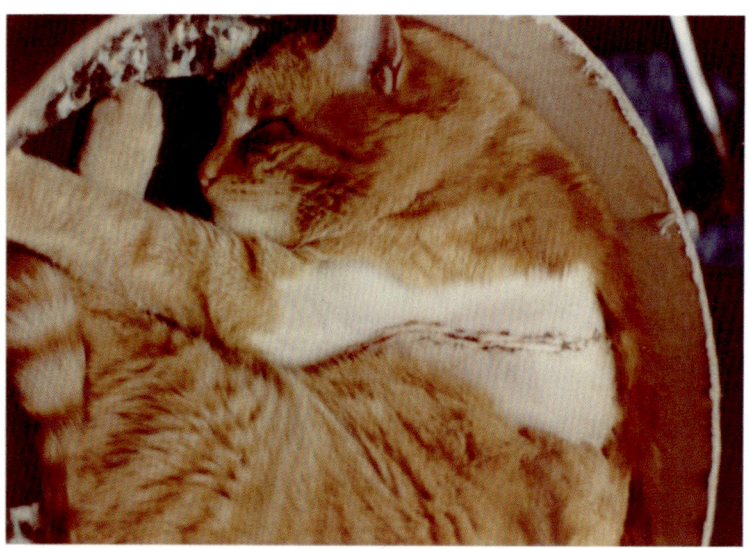

Recuperating after Surgery

RUBBERPLANT SURVIVAL

Rubber plants are native to eastern and south Asia, but they have become a favorite houseplant in Europe and North America. They are beautiful tree-like plant with waxy dark green leaves that are rubbery in appearance. Known for their great height, they are easy to care for and generally fast growing.

However, they are very toxic to pets. Thankfully, Tiger showed no interest whatsoever in any of our houseplants

As a housewarming gift, friends brought us a grand rubber-tree, about four feet tall, in a very attractive pot. The vaulted center of our living-room was 16 feet height, and we placed the tree near the big living-room window and sliding balcony door, in direct sunlight.

I pampered this fabulous plant, watered every Monday and added water soluble fertilizer every other week. I also wiped the leaves with a damp cloth, which I dipped into a 50/50 milk-and-water solution to ensure that the leaves continue to be healthy and shiny.

This awesome rubber tree soon grew to be 10 feet height and 9 feet wide. Its majestic size completed the decor of our living-room, and it became a conversation piece with our friends and family.

In the winter, we always had dinner and card parties with friends. On one of those occasions, on an extremely cold winter evening, it was our turn to have friends over. Long before our guest arrived, our teenage sons took their dinner plates downstairs to the family room to watch a movie.

Several dinner guests arrived early and seated themselves at the dinner table. Dennis served drinks, while I prepared to serve the dinner. I remember that I had baked a big salmon, wrapped in foil with butter, lemon, garlic, onion with herbs, and I served it with wild rice, carrots and green salad. Then for dessert, we had a delicious German cheesecake.

The meal was definitely a success, but while we were eating the desert, I was abruptly embarrassed.

Our friend Jacky jokingly remarked: "No wonder your rubber plant grows like a weed, with the watering it gets."

I was flabbergasted! There was Tiger sitting in the rubber plant pot and peeing. He even covered it up, just like he did in his kitty litter box.

Our guests were all amused, but to me it was not a laughing matter. I chased Tiger downstairs, and then I realized that the boys had closed the door to the TV room so as not to hear the noise from upstairs. Therefore, Tiger was unable to reach his litter box, which was located downstairs in the laundry-room.

Our friends left around midnight. Then our job began, as we could not leave the rubber plant overnight as it was. Cats urine burns the roots of plants and does a lot of harm. So, the rubber plant would have to be hosed down with water, but in the living room that was impossible.

Dennis laid out a tarp on the floor, and we scooped most of soil out of the pot, then we poured warm water over the remaining soil to dilute the rest of the cat's urine. The rubber plant was already secured with tall bamboo poles, but now it had to be hand-held straight up for support.

We always bought several large bags of potting soil, and luckily, we still had two bags in stock. Dennis added the soil into the pot, and then he added a gallon of water with fertilizing solution. Fortunately, there was no harm done to the rubber tree, and two years later it reached 12 feet in height and 10 feet across.

Meanwhile, Norcan Construction had just completed the BC Forestry Office, 20 km from where we lived. It had an elaborate entrance with an open lobby that was two floors high with tall windows and a fancy stairway that lead to the Forestry offices. So, this was just the right place for our Rubber-tree. It was admired by the visitors who entered the building, and they often asked the staff how they got such a gigantic plant into the building and where did it come from?

When Norcan bought our rubber plant, they built a special container for its delivery. To remove the plant from our living room, it had to be carried out of the living room balcony door, over the balcony railing of the second floor of the house, and then hoisted down unto a large truck. It was then transported in its container to town. Four men were responsible for the transfer.

I decided not to grow another rubber plant. Smaller plants are much easier to deal with.

HUMMINGBIRDS

The Calliope Hummingbird is the tiniest of the five humming-bird's species found in central interior British Columbia and southwestern Alberta.

The so- called Rufous, or Ruby Throated hummingbird, also called the black-chinned hummingbird (the smallest of the North American Hummingbirds) live during summer as far north then as Prince George. The birds always come back to their old nesting side.

Some hummingbirds stay all winter at the lower Mainland of British Columbia, and others migrate every Spring from California or Mexico to British Columbia and Alberta. NO, they do not migrate on the back of the Canada Geese. The small hummers flap their wings 55 – 200 times per seconds, and, on average, they live five or six years in the wild.

Hummingbirds have a very high metabolism, and a great deal of energy is spent flying. They have to eat constantly, and they consume half their body weight every day, feeding primarily on flower nectar and soft bodied insects - mainly mosquitoes. They lap nectar with their sticky tongues. They also feed on sugar water they find at Hummingbird feeders, when no flowers are in bloom yet.

Because hummingbirds fly so much, they have poorly developed feed and they can barely walk. Instead, they are able to perch on a feeder. They can fly forward or backwards, shift sideways, or suddenly stop in midair.

Knowing that the Hummingbirds are extremely territorial, I hung two feeders out of side of each other. I made the solution to fill the feeders - four parts water and one-part sugar. One feeder I hung from a branch that was close to the trunk of a pine tree, which was easily visible from the kitchen window. Then I hung a second feeder on the balcony railing of the second story of the house.

One sunny morning, Tiger sat near the pine tree watching Hummingbirds come and go from the feeding station. Then, all of a sudden, he climbed up the tree trunk, most likely wishing that one of those birdies would fly into his mouth. Tiger's paws had to keep a strong grip on to the trunk so he wouldn't fall. While he patiently waited for a bird fly towards him, the sticky sweet sugar water tripped down on his paws, on his head and into his eyes, and also down his back. What the heck, this was not working, so he climbed down the tree and walked away.

It took my cat almost all afternoon washing and grooming himself to get rid of the nasty sugar water that had messed up his shiny fur coat.

The next morning, while I was working in the kitchen, I looked out the window and admired several Hummingbirds hovering around the feeder. Four birds were sitting on the perch sucking on the sweet fluid, while others were flying back and forth waiting for their turn to drink.

Tiger sat on the ground about ten feed away from the tree trunk and the feeder, observing the Hummingbirds having their fill. Somehow, I had a feeling that he was up to no good. And sure enough!!

Tiger skillfully made a giant leap into mid-air and grabbed a hummer in mid-flight as it was leaving the feeding station. I screamed out of the kitchen widow: "Tiger, NO NO NO!"

Tiger dropped the bird, and it flew away. Then ten minutes later, the same drama! Again, I screamed, Tiger let go of the bird and the bird flew off.

By now I had enough, and I ran downstairs and outside to rescue the birds that were using the feeder. However, when I finally reached the feeder, my cat already had another Hummingbird in his mouth. He took one look at me, as I ferociously yelled at him, and then he dropped the bird to the ground and he ran off.

I picked up the bird, holding it softly in my warm hand. It showed no wounds, no bite marks - its whole body was intact. The bird's eyes were closed, and I was certain that it had perished. Then after a few minutes, I felt movement in my hand, and the eyes of the bird opened and stared at me. He must have been just in shock.

With my left hand, I unhooked the feeder from the tree, while still holding on to the bird with my right hand. I then placed the bird onto one of the feeder's perches. Surprise - the bird just set there to collect itself, and then drank from the feeder. It sat there for another few minutes resting, and then flew away. It was his lucky day.

During the time I was holding the feeder, I didn't make a move and held my breath. Other Hummingbirds came to drink at the same time. They totally ignored me standing there. It was a wonderful feeling just to be part of their scenery.

How did Tiger get to the point of catching Hummingbirds?. He must have noticed that the birds were heavier after feeding. Then he must estimate the distance the birds would fly after feeding and how low they would zoom down with their increased body weight. The birds were then an easy catch.

To be safe I hung the feeder outside the kitchen window, which was off the second floor of the house. Tiger never caught another Hummingbird.

BILLY THE GOAT

Country living has its challenges. Every year, from spring until late fall, I would ride my bike once a week to my neighbor's place on Beaverly Road to buy fresh eggs. The Davidson's raise free-range chickens, which means the small flock of chickens roam their property freely without being fenced in, and they are fed outdoors. So, they spend the day wandering around, drinking from their water bowl, or laying eggs in the shed. Then for safety, the chickens are kept in a closed shed overnight.

Opposite our property was Robinson's Horse Stable and Riding School, where they used to board horses month-to-month. On the wall in the stable were fancy riding saddles with all kinds of accessories, and there was a daily schedule for training the horses.

Behind the barn was a large property with fences and a riding arena with all kinds of horse training equipment. Beside the arena was a large pasture where the horses could happily grace.

Every morning the stalls were cleaned, and the maintenance man had the task of keeping the stable in good condition. I watched him as he removed the wet straw from the barn to replace it with fresh straw. He piled the old straw with a pitchfork unto a big pile beside the road, from where it was later removed. Meanwhile a billy goat followed the man back and forth to and from the barn, and he clearly enjoyed jumping on top of the stinky pile of straw.

One morning as I was cycling home from buying fresh eggs, the billy goat was standing in the middle of the road. He clearly had no intention of moving, so I jumped off my bike and walked towards him. I called to the man who was standing beside the barn watching me, and asked if the goat was friendly? He laughed and replied: "His name is Billy; he loves people and he's treated like a pet." So I scratched Billy's forehead, which he seemed to enjoy.

As I proceeded on my journey home, a galloping noise followed me. Billy was chasing after my bike. The faster I peddled, the faster he ran. I had to pass my house in order to go into the garage and park my bike. Then trying to get from the garage to my house was a challenge, as for every step I took, Billy took three steps towards me. He would lower his head, charging at me with his horns, and thus chase me back into the garage. A spade became my defense weapon and I swung it around while running to my house.

At the house, I immediately phoned Billy's owner and begged her to come and get her goat. Mrs. Robinson's response was that I should keep Billy, and she assured me that he would be a great addition to my family. I told her that I had no interest whatsoever in owning a billy goat, and especially one that wanted to chase me.

My dogs and my cat had been put in the house when I left for my bike ride, and now they had to stay put until Billy was gone.

Ginger and Joey had watched my ordeal with Billy, and both dogs had barked ferociously through a partly open window above. The goat looked up at the dogs and then went on with what he was doing, which was destroying my flowers and bushes.

Several times I opened the front door, and each time, like a raging bull, the goat thumped into the closed door.

Tiger, who usually took cat naps during the day, awoke due to the noise of the barking dogs. Now there were two dogs and a cat charging from the window towards the unwanted invader below.

I opened the living-room balcony door, to observe how much damage had been done to my rockery garden. Billy stood right on the top of it, nibbling happily. Tiger followed me, and then jumped unto the balcony railing. Luckily I was able to hold him back. He had been about to take a gigantic leap off the second floor to take charge of Billy.

Tiger's fur fluffed up to twice its size, including his bushy tail. He was hissing and growling fearlessly and the goat stopped eating and looked up at Tiger. If Tiger had gotten hold of Billy, it would not have ended well. I am certain that Tiger would have severely scratched the goat's face.

Tiger never backed away from danger and he was super-fast. One day Tiger brought home a dead weasel, that he had killed. He never ate his kills, and as always, he brought his prey home to show off his skill.

Three hours passed while I watched desperately from my balcony as this sure-footed buck was on my rockery garden, d-rooting all my plants and eating some of them. He also ventured around the back of the house, nicked all the gladiolas and dahlias, and ate the lush green shrubs. And all the flower pots were up-rooted.

Outraged, I phoned my neighbor again. I told what damage Billy had done and that she would be charged for the cost.

She came shortly after my call, carrying a dog collar and a leash. She looked around our yard at the devastation, said nothing, and then left with Billy on a leash. He walked beside her like a well-trained, obedient dog.

I was glad that my boys were at school that day. If they hadn't been, they certainly would have begged me to keep Billy the goat.

A few months later, a neighbor told me, that Billy had charged a horse owner who was visiting the riding stable. The goat was then given to a farmer further out of town, and apparently, he lived a happy life with other goats.

My job was to nurse all my plant back to their former health and beauty.

That summer I invested hundreds of dollars on flowers, potted plants and shrubs from a nursery. I wanted my property to look beautiful because my brother and his family were going to be visiting us from Germany.

However, it was all to no avail, - I picked up our visitors at the Vancouver airport and we drove back to Prince George, arriving home on July3rd. While I was away, there had been a heavy early night frost (very rare in July), and as I drove into our yard, I could see that all the plants were frostbitten, wilted or black.

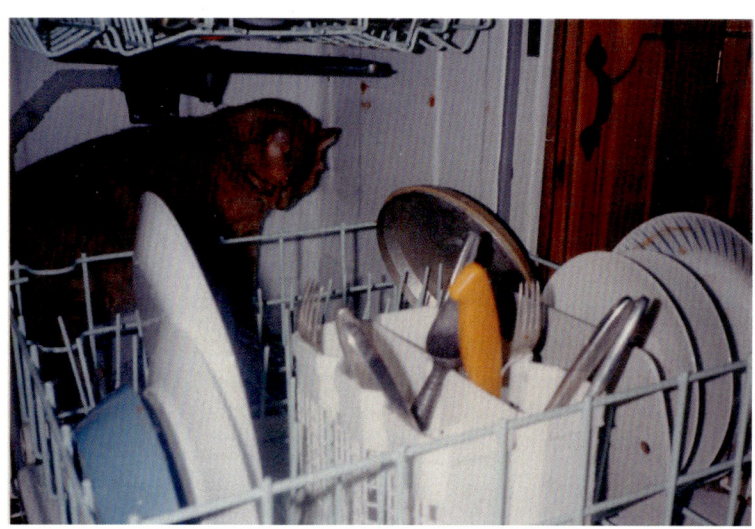

TIGER AND THE NEW VACUUM CLEANER

Our Sears Kenmore vacuum was a good vacuum for 10 years but it did not have the strength for the thick shag carpets that were in style in the 70's and installed in most houses.

We purchased a more powerful Electrolux vacuum cleaner, and never did I imagine that this would traumatize our beloved Tiger.

As a kitten he was brought up with every possible machine noise in our household, and he was never afraid of anything. Tiger loved a total body rub with the vacuum cleaner, and he would lay on his back while I used a small brush attachment to sweep over his entire body. Other times we had fun when I vacuumed the kitchen floor while Tiger was eating from his bowl, and I would suck his tail into the hose of the vacuum cleaner. Tiger just kept eating, and he would eat by making a sound like 'num-numnum', while his tail was in the vacuum suction. Nothing could ever disturb his dinner. But then we were talking about the old Kenmore vacuum cleaner with little suction.

Every Friday, while I was at work, Eve cleaned and vacuumed our house. On this particular Friday, I phoned her to let her know that a new vacuum cleaner was sitting on the living-room floor ready for her to use. She and Tiger had always gotten along well, and there had never been an issue – except when Eve tried to use the new Electrolux.

There was a frantic phone call from Eve while I was at work, thanking me for the lovely new vacuum cleaner, but asking for the old Kenmore back, because Tiger would not allow her to use the new Electrolux.

Apparently, Tiger physically attacked the new vacuum cleaner whenever Eve tried to move it back and forth. After Eve had shut off the motor, Tiger was still clinging onto the top part of the vacuum cleaner and insisting that he wanted it to stay there – by hissing at Eve if she came near him. It was clear that he was a persistent cat with a definite attitude regarding the new vacuum cleaner. Eve got out the old Kenmore and finished her job, and then Tiger was content for the rest of that day.

I had to deal with the new vacuum cleaner problem on my off-days. The new vacuum stayed in the middle of the living-room floor. Several times during the day, Tiger would walk up to it and sniff it all over, as if it was a foreign body that did not belong here in our house. I started the motor every few hours for a few minutes, but if I tried to move it, Tiger would hiss at it. Eventually, he would sit on top of the long body of the Electrolux, growling and hissing when the motor started again, while I tried to move slowly around.

On the third day, Tiger realized the vacuum cleaner was here to stay.

Then the following week, I attached a small brush and gently moved it over his back – he loved it! From then on, he expected to be vacuum-brushed whenever one of us cleaned the floor. Eve never experienced another hissy fit with Tiger, and she never forgot to give Tiger a vacuum-brush before she started cleaning.

Tiger's tail was never sucked into the new hose of the Electrolux, as it was too powerful of a motor.

MILA THE NEW PUPPY

After the sudden passing of Ginger, who had suffered a massive stroke, Tiger and Joey were at a loss. They were sad and Joey howled for days. Tiger just stayed home close to me, as if he were waiting for Ginger to come back.

He never crossed the road to the other field to hunt for mice by himself, so he was missing his hunting buddy. He just sat with Joey outside, and it was another boring day. We all mourned Ginger - she was such a beautiful and loyal dog, and left us too soon.

A month later, I visited a girlfriend, Marlene, who had just bought the cutest black and white English Springer Spaniel puppy. Marlene also had a young Calico kitten that was extremely funny and active. The kitten would sit on the stairway and wait for the puppy to walk by. Then she would jump on the puppy and they would wrestle on the floor, obviously enjoying themselves. They were made for each other, and we enjoyed every minute of the entertainment.

Marlene told me that the owner of the puppy has one left, so I phoned the lady immediately and she agreed to see me and my boys the next day. She gave me directions to her house over the phone because they lived far out of town, and she told me to bring $200 for the puppy.

When we arrived, we entered a lovely courtyard. And there was Tika, the most beautiful looking mama dog of the puppies, relaxing in the sun on the front lawn. She had separated herself from her last puppy, which was now three months old. A friendly, young lady, Andrea, met us at the front door and walked us into the living-room to see the puppy. Mila was black and white in color and a beauty like her mom. She playfully interacted with my teenage boys as if they were already good friends.

I phoned my husband to let him know that we are bringing the new puppy home, and this time he agreed. The boys and I were ecstatic to have a new friend for Joey and Tiger. On the way home, Michael sat on the back seat of the car trying to hold Mila in his arms, but she was all play. She seemed totally unconcerned that she was on a car ride and separated from her mom and home.

When we arrived home, Joey was standing in the front yard, waving his tail with excitement as he saw us. I tried to hold Mila back, but she jumped from my hands and ran to Joey to greet him as if they were long-lost friends.

Joey did not know what to make of this, but clearly liked Mila. She constantly jumped up at him, while he was walking around, and it seemed that they had already bonded. Joey started to run in circles and little Mila followed him everywhere. Black Labrador Retrievers are known to be a very friendly dog that gets along well with other canines. This was Joey for sure, and he helped Mila to adjust and never get homesick.

Dennis came outside to greet our newcomer, and he too loved Mila at first sight. She instantly ran to him when he called her name, and we all agreed that we are lucky to have found such a smart and friendly puppy.

Now came the first hurdle. Tiger, our guarding cat, was not impressed with the new arrival. He was already waiting inside the front entrance for us to come in and his fur was all standing on end, including his tail. He made himself look twice his size, or so he thought. And as usual, he ran to the seventh step of the stairway, thus letting us know that Mila was not allowed to pass. Mila, however, was too fast for him. Springer Spaniels leap into the air like a deer and, she jumped like a bullet over Tiger and ran into the kitchen. Joey came to her side, but he was not able to be a good protector for the puppy.

Tiger chased Mila into a corner, lashing at her with his paws. Dennis came to Mila's rescue, lifted her up and holding her in his arms. Tiger stood in front of Dennis hissing and growling as he looked up at Mila, and poor little Mila whined. She could not understand, why this dangerous animal was being so mean to her. She wanted to love Tiger, but he would not budge.

It was funny to watch, but not a good situation. Tiger was now six years old and a conscientious watch dog, or so he thought. So, we put his bed downstairs in the family room. It was a must to keep him separated from the puppy.

As I worked in the yard to winterize it, Mila and Joey enjoyed being outside with me. They played all day and always slept together, and they adored each other. Joey had been neutered as a puppy, but Mila was not spayed as we expected her to have one litter of puppies in later years. It was not a problem, when she was in heat. Living on an acreage was safe for her, and Joey was not interested, which was a great relieve for us and for Mila.

As the weather got colder, the pets had to stay inside more. Tiger still did not accept Mila, and most likely she would never replace Ginger. As for Mila, she stayed very close to Joey. This was perfect because the doctor's order was to keep Joey indoors more so he could stay warm. Joey was now ten years old, suffered from severe arthritis and moved very slowly, and the doctor had prescribed medication for pain.

Mila cuddled up to Joey, when he was lying on his bed, and he enjoyed the attention. Mila was a very gentle dog, and most of the time she pulled on Joey's waging tail. I bought her several toys to play with, but her favorite toys were old used tennis balls - which she carried in her mouth most of the day.

If visitors drove into our yard Mila would run to greet them by throwing her ball at them, hoping that they would throw it into the air for her to catch. She had become addicted to her game, and she always caught her ball in mid-air.

Both pets were fed twice a day, and every day I moved Mila's dish a little closer to Tiger. If Mila came too close to him, he would smack her, but not using his claws. By now, Mila had grown taller than Tiger and weighed about the same as he did.

When it comes to food, cats are not like dogs; they have very different eating habits. Cats always leave food in their dish for later.

Joey was an enthusiastic eater, and he would always gobble up his food as soon as I put it down for him. But as he grew older his appetite changed, and he wasn't as excited about mealtimes.

Mila was a very delicate eater, except if Tiger left food in his dish. Then she would snick into the kitchen and eat his leftovers. If he caught her eating his food, he would beat her up. But obviously did not care because she would still steal his food regularly.

Tiger beat up Mila too much. But she became faster, smarter and much bigger than him, and then she really surprised him one day. The kitchen floor was newly washed and waxed, and too slippery for Tiger to run away. Now it was Mila's turn to put Tiger in his place, she must have decided that she was fed up with being bossed around.

As he was eating his evening meal, Mila was sneaking behind his back in slow motion, but he did not notice her. She grabbed him by his shoulder and shook him violently. What a racket of noise growling and crying! Tiger was flabbergasted but not hurt.

I watched the whole ordeal as I was working at the kitchen sink. I had waited for this moment to happen for a long time, knowing that it would. Both creatures respected each other from that day on, and Tiger never bossed Mila around or lashed out at her again.

Tiger still had one advantage when it came to controlling Mila. If her ball ended up near him, he would sit for the longest time beside it. Then, if Mila tried to get her ball, Tiger would put his front paw over the ball, and then hiss and growl at her. She would then bark at him until he gave up and walked away. This was a daily ritual - their all-time favorite game.

Mila attended obedience class for three years, starting as a puppy and finally completing the advanced training. She was best in all the activities. It was easy and fun to train her and she always wanted to please me. Then there was playtime after class. Mila was naturally social, and she easily accepted new people and new dogs - and also other species.

Mila scored well at a Licensed Obedience Trail with the Northern Interior Kennel Club. She brought home one silver and three gold medals, and we were very proud of her. She was truly an awesome dog.

Mila and Tiger – Stand-off!

FOND MEMORIES OF TIGER

In a sense, I truly believe that Tiger was a clown.

Tiger always enjoyed a good back-rub, or being padded on his forehead. He would sit anytime in front of me, or us, and expect to be stroked on his forehead.

I, or someone else, would smooth his hair on his head backwards and then stroke it forward, so it looked like a crew-cut, with the hair on his head standing up. Then Tiger would lay his ears flat backwards and his pupils would enlarge, and we would know that Tiger is ready for an ambush. He then would jump and attack our legs from the front and bite into our pant legs. This game he only played during the winter in lock-down - anything to get our attention, and we always had fun.

Other times, the boys would run through the house chasing after Tiger, but he was extremely fast, and he would run far ahead of them, only to hide around a corner until the boys were running past him... Then he would ambush them from the back and jumped up on their legs, and bite them through their pants. Then he would jump off them and the game would be reversed, because he would chase the boys and then again stop around the corner waiting for them to come running back. Then he jumped on them and pulled on their pant leg. This too was a winter indoor entertainment.

For relaxation and creativity, knitting had been my favorite hobby from a very young age. Most of the sweaters that the members of my family wore had been created by me. I always secured my knitting, and a job in progress would go into a basked with a lid, and I would store it in a safe place whenever I finished knitting for that day. But sometimes I would answer the phone or be otherwise occupied and leave my knitting laying on the chair. Then I would totally forget about Tiger being in the room, and when I returned to my chair, I would see that my cat had vandalized my artwork.

Tiger would remove the knitting needles from the unfinished part. He then would pull on the yarn and pull the knitted piece apart. Often his nails would get tangled in the wool and then he had to fight to free himself by destroying the knitting beyond repair. Or he would knead his paws into the knitting, and then lay on it to sleep - oh, it was so soft.

Those were moments when I would be furious with my crazy cat, but of course it was my mistake to leave my knitting unattended when Tiger was around.

James lived with us during the time of his teacher's practicum, and he had been with us for several weeks. Tiger caused him no problem whenever we were home as a family.

James' working hours were different from the boys' school hours, and also from Dennis' and my work schedule. Often, he would come home early, and then he would experience a rude welcome from Tiger. Our cat again would sit on the seventh step and refuse to let James go upstairs. He would do his usual growling and hissing, also lashing out with his paws. For protection James would hold his briefcase up to his face and chest and proceed upstairs. He knew, that Tiger meant to be a very aggressive, impersonating a guard dog. This episode went on daily during the week. On weekends Tiger tolerated James as part of our family, but James never trusted the cat, regardless how charming Tiger could be.

On one of my off-days, I came home after shopping and Tiger was sitting on his seventh step, not making a move. Apparently, he was just washing his rear end and I thought that he was sitting on a white piece of thread. I thought I would pick it up, not realizing what it was. As I held on to it, Tiger ran upstairs letting out a painful cry. I had pulled on a string that came out of his rectum.

A closer look, and I realized it was a long dental floss that Tiger had swallowed and then most like tried to get it out for himself. When I noticed the thread he was sitting on, it was about 4 inches out of his butt.

Because the floss was bloody, I rushed Tiger to the vet, believing that I had done harm to my cat. Dr.

Thomas assured me that Tiger was okay, and he smiled and said: "Tiger comes to see me for the darnedest injuries, he is the most adventurous and daring cat".

Later I noticed that the downstairs bathroom door was typically kept open and that Tiger liked to entertain himself by turning over the waste basket. The problem was that it would often contain used dental floss, which Tiger would then consume. A lesson learned - to keep every bathroom door in our house closed at all times.

MOVING FROM BEAVERLY RD TO RIVERVIEW RD.

Leaving the Beaverly home was not easy; but moving to Riverview road was a great decision. The children had grown and left the home they grew up in, so the country home became too big. We had lived on 15 acre of land, 16 km from town, and now we had moved to a smaller house on a half-acre of property, 7 km from town. Winter driving was less dangerous, and I enjoyed being closer to town.

The mover had left, and everything valuable had been packed in boxes and placed into my small hatchback car. Some boxes were piled in the back seat, and then Tiger in his kennel was securely placed on top of the boxes.

Joey rode in Dennis' truck to our new home because there was no room for him in my car.

Mila was sitting on the front passenger seat. I had not yet driven out of our driveway when Tiger frantically started crying in his kennel. Mila instantly jumped onto the console between the front seats and with her front paws shook the kennel and she growled at

Tiger at the same time. Tiger was so flabbergasted that he was quiet for the entire trip to our new home.

The dogs settled immediately into the new environment, but not Tiger. He disappeared into a bedroom and then only appeared for meals, or using his kitty litter box. This went on for five days. On the fifth evening, Tiger stood in front of the balcony sliding door, wanting to go outside, and I let him out. What was I thinking? - it was nighttime! Tiger was a no-show for that night and the following night.

We were worried sick, and we walked up and down the road calling for Tiger, but no luck. Our new neighbor asked what we were looking for, and when we explained our situation, he made a remark about not letting the cat or dogs out at night because coyotes were roaming the neighborhood. That really made me feel good...!

On the third evening, Tiger was suddenly sitting outside the balcony door, I let him in with a huge sigh of relief, but for him it was like he had never left. He was very hungry but calm, and he never went into hiding again. It was just like he had lived here before.

This mild behavior definitely puzzled me - but not Dennis. My husband believed that Tiger had walked along the river bank, maybe trying to walk back to his old house. And then when he could not find a way to cross the river, (even though there was the foothill bridge over the Nechako river nearby), he must have realized that there was no way to get back to the old homestead, and so he ventured back to his new home instead.

After that he stayed close to me, and wherever I went, he followed me around, inside the house or on the property. And he never left our property again for as long as we lived there.

JOEY'S DEPARTURE

In the Fall of 1989, I visited my family in Germany, and after my return home to Canada, I struggled with the nine-hours' time difference between Europe and Canada.

So, I could not sleep at night, and one night when I went to the kitchen for a glass of water, I noticed that Mila was sleeping by herself in her bed. Joey and Mila never slept apart, so I was concerned! I was sneaking around the house, trying not to wake my husband, as I looked for Joey. I found him downstairs in the family room lying under the pool table. He just wagged his tail and moaned painfully, and he did not want to get up! So, I covered him with a blanked to keep him warm for the night.

Early next morning, I walked Joey from the family room (to prevent for him using the stairway, which would have caused him enormous pain) through the garage and outside the house so he could urinate. He had trouble standing on his three legs. Then I walked him to my car and drove straight to the vet clinic, where Dr. Thomas said he would keep our dog in the clinic for some blood tests and for an abdominal x-ray.

Of course, Joey was in good hands, but I was very worried about the outcome. I drove to work early that day, and soon after I entered the office, I received a phone call from the vet. He explained to me that Joey had a 7-inch tumor in his intestine. I remembered that for the past few months, Joey would always moan whenever he lay down. Dennis and I presumed that this was due to the dog's arthritis. He had been diagnosed with arthritis the year before and it was somewhat controlled with medication that the vet had prescribed.

Because Joey was in his twelfth year and in excruciating pain, the Doctor advised us to have him humanely euthanized and therefore end his suffering. Dennis and I had no time to say good-bye, but sadly we gave the okay because we felt it was best for our beloved dog.

Joey's death was very upsetting for us, but even more so for our dog Mila, who had never in all her lifetime spent a moment without Joey. Joey had kept her out of trouble when she was growing up and doing what puppies do best, which is damaging things.

The time had come for Tiger, our cat, to accept Mila the dog as her friend, so as to overcome her loneliness during the night. They grew closer every day and eventually lived in peace together. No more maliciousness from Tiger aimed at Mila, and that was a good thing for both of them!

Across the street from our house lived a young couple with two boys and a lovely two-year-old Golden Retriever named Dusty. Every time the owner took Dusty outside and tied him to a long leash, he would howl loudly. The couple worked and the boys went to school, so Dusty had severe separation anxiety, even when he was left in the house by himself.

When Joey was still with us, we would take our dogs on walks and we got to know each other quite well. After they heard about Joey's passing, they phoned us and asked if Mila could stay with Dusty during the day. And that solved the problem for all of us. Tiger would not miss Mila during the day because he napped all day; He had become an old senior cat.

My work started at 12:30 p.m. My neighbor was a teacher, and she left at 8:00 a.m. and was home by

3:30 p.m. She would leave Dusty in the house, and before I left for work, I would let him out and tie him to his long leash. Mila would join him, and she was not tied down because she would never leave the site. I left them water, treats and chew toys, and they had fun playing together.

If the weather was not perfect, I would walk the dogs and then leave them together in Dusty's house in a designated area. Dusty could not come to our house, because our fierce Tiger would beat him up. Dusty had tried previously to be Tiger's friend, but Tiger would just hiss at him and lash out with his front paws.

At 3:30 p.m., after school, the boys would take the two dogs for a walk and then let them into their house. I would come home from work around 6:30 p.m. Mila would sit in Dusty's house in the hallway, and whenever she heard our electric garage door open, she would bark inside their front door so they let her out and she could run home. She was always excited to see me.

Sometimes on Saturday's, Mila would run over to Dusty's place when he was outside and she would play with him for hours. And she knew that she would always get treats when she was there.

When we moved to Shuswap Lake, we became friends with our new neighbor's down the road from us, and we often played cards. Mila would always be with us when we visited, and she would always get a treat. The Simpson's always had treats available for when visitors came with their dog.

Mila was smart, and once in a while, she would run down the road to the Simpsons and bark at their front door. The first time Mila did that, Glade phoned me and said: "Mila is here and she is barking up a storm. Are you okay?

"We are fine," I said. "I'll bet she is begging you for a treat and then she will run back home."

Sure enough, this was the case, and it was repeated many times over the following five years, as long as Mila was with us. It was fun for all of us...Living on a gravel road and on a quiet cul-de-sac, in the countryside meant that it was safe for Mila to run back and forth. Mila and Tiger got themselves quite a reputation, but they were loved by all our neighbors.

Sometimes Tiger would run with Mila halfway, and then he would sit by the road in the deep grass and wait for her return from the neighbors, so he could walk back home with her.

Joey and Mila

SNATCHED BY A FOX

The winter of 1990 had been exceptionally harsh in Prince George, and Tiger had not set foot outside during the cold and snowy season.

But by mid-April some of the snow had finally melted, and the days were longer, sunnier, and warmer.

Over a period of four weeks, the neighbors kept knocking at our front door and asking if our cat was still around...?

The story was: The neighbors' beloved cats were disappearing one by one. A pair of foxes had conveniently built a den at the bottom of the Nechako riverbank, and a silver fox was roaming around the neighborhood searching for food. Obvious, domestic cats were an easy catch.

Foxes usually do not pose a danger to cats or small dogs, but this winter was definitely colder, snowier, and longer than usual. Due to the very deep snow, they were not able to hunt for rodents like mice and rats. If possible, they also hunt for rabbits, marmots and gophers, if they can find them.

I had seen several silver foxes on top of the riverbank, or running across the road. Their thick coat has a silvery appearance and the tip of the tail is white. Silver foxes are only found in the northern part of British Columbia, Yukon and Alaska.

That early spring, four adorable silver fox cubs emerged slowly and ever so careful from their den. They looked almost black in appearance. Most likely they had been left to themselves for a short time.

Mid-March is the peak period when vixen usually gives birth to four or five cubs, and they stay with their mother in the den for about three weeks: and then she still continues to nurse them until they are about two months old. Fox parents take great care of their young.

The newborn cubs are deaf, blind and unable to thermo-regulate for the first two weeks, so their mother rarely leaves them. After two weeks, the kits open their eyes, and they also start to hear. Meanwhile the male fox brings food for his female partner – which is the first sign that a den is occupied.

In mid-April of that year, some of our relatives came visiting for a week, including for the spring school-break and Easter. With four little youngsters running and playing throughout our home, Tiger basically stayed out of sight. He was not used to extreme noise, but I refused to let him outside, since I had been told of the danger.

As I was preparing our Easter-Sunday dinner, Tiger, without me noticing was sitting at the balcony sliding door hoping to be let out. One of the guests opened the door and let the cat out. After dinner, I called Tiger to feed him, and my son told me that someone had let Tiger out earlier. We ran outside calling his name, but there was no sign of him. Usually he returned my calls with "Ma-Maa", whenever I wanted him to come home.

Nightfall was around 5:30 p.m. There was still snow on the ground and it was not easy to venture behind buildings, plus there were only a few street-lights. We were not able to find Tiger.

Worried about my cat, I stayed up all night, hoping that Tiger would appear at the balcony door. Then morning came and went, and there was no sign of him.

It was early morning on Easter Monday when our guests departed to drive home. Needless to say, that I was happy to be alone with my husband, for me to be able to mourn my ever-loving Tiger. I felt sick to my stomach just to think of what Tiger had to endure to be a fox's meal.

I phoned my neighbors to ask them to please keep a lookout for Tiger. Some had lost their cats earlier to a fox, but no one believed that our 24-pound tabby would fall prey to a fox, because he was a vicious fighter and fast. During the day we walked around the neighborhood and down to the riverbank, this time of the year the river is very low. There was no trace of Tiger. We even approached the foxes' den under a wooded area that was thick with underbrush. The fox family had vanished. Probably they had been disturbed by us and by other humans searching for their cats. Foxes are known to build several dens, so as to rear the young safely, and they will carry their kits from den to den.

There was no sign of Tiger's fur in the den. I was certain, that Tiger would have been snatched from the back and had most likely fought for his life. And during the fight the fox might have suffered serious injuries from Tiger's claws and teeth. Whenever Tiger had to defend himself he made lot of noise and made himself looking twice the size.

Then two evenings had passed since Tiger's disappearance. We ate left-overs for supper, and then Dennis and I retired to the family room to watch a good movie on TV, just to get our mind off our missing cat.

Halfway through the movie, I got up to get us a drink and a snack from the kitchen, when all of a sudden I heard a cat crying at the balcony door, it was Tiger! And, he was frantically trying to get into the house. It was not his usual deep voice, but rather a high pitched cry. This he did only if he was in pain, so it alarmed me!

Tears ran down Dennis', and my face; no-one would ever understand how we felt, the joy of having our beloved cat back was overwhelming, but short lived.

I tried to lift him up, but he refused to be held. His body looked completely intact, without a scratch mark or any signs of blood. His fur had always been very thick. He just showed me the door to go downstairs, he ran straight to his litter-box to relieve himself. In the meantime, I filled his food and water dish and placed it nearby his bed, thinking that he might be too exhausted from what he had experienced, he needed a good rest.

Before going to bed, I checked on Tiger, to see how he was doing. To my shock, he was not in his bed. His food was untouched, but he had drunk a lot of water. Dennis and I called him, but he did not show up. We searched throughout the entire house until Dennis found him hiding in the dark behind the heater in the sauna room. Dennis lifted Tiger up to check him over, and Tiger cried out in pain. Then Dennis noticed a severe swelling above his pelvis on the left side.

Early the next morning, we rushed Tiger to the veterinarian clinic. During the night he had developed a high fever, a sure sign of infection. The vet examined Tiger, he sedated him, and then shaved his hind leg and pelvis. Tiger had suffered severe bite wounds, ripping his pelvis up to his back, and there was a large abscess with a lot of pus.

A lab test proved that this had been caused by a bacterial infection, almost life-threatening, with a buildup of pus inside the wound. Luckily, Tiger was up-to-date with his rabies vaccine.

Our tough Tabby needed surgery and he once again had to have extended lacerations.

We left the clinic knowing that Tiger was in good hands. After surgery he was kept in the clinic for another three days, and then we finally received a phone-call to pick him up. We were ushered into a waiting room, and our cat was brought in for me to hold. There were extensive lacerations, all sutured up, and a temporary rubber tube for fluid drainage had been inserted. And Tiger needed to wear a neck collar to prevent him from licking his wounds.

The Doctor consulted with us as to how to take good care of our furry baby. Then it was my job to nurse Tiger back to good health, and to give him his pain medication and antibiotics.

I had to keep the wounded area clean and dry, and remove any debris discharging from the drainage tube. I washed it with cotton balls doused in warm water. I did this on a regular basis, and after eight days, the drainage stopped oozing.

My cat was a perfect patient. He had been in terrible conditions before, and he knew that as his parent, I would make him well again. He never rejected his medication.

I would bring his food bowl to his bed, then hold it for him so he could eat his meal, and the same for drinking water.

However, going to the litter box was an entirely different matter. As I said before, Tiger could change his voice, and when he needed the litter box, he used his hoarse voice to call me: Ma...Maa. Then I would pick him up and carry him wrapped in a towel to his kitty litter box. I would set him down beside it, and he would watch me scratching a hole with a bent old fork. Then I would place him on the opening to relieve himself. After, I placed him beside the litter box again, he would watch me covering up his debris with clean litter. This procedure was done three times daily.

It never failed: while Tiger was being carried back to his bed, he always licked my cheeks and gently bit my ear, as if to say: "Thank you, mom." I know for fact the he truly appreciated me helping him with his recovery, which took several weeks until finally the ordeal was over.

Tiger stayed close to home all summer, and he never ventured outside in the winter again for as long as we lived in Prince George, BC.

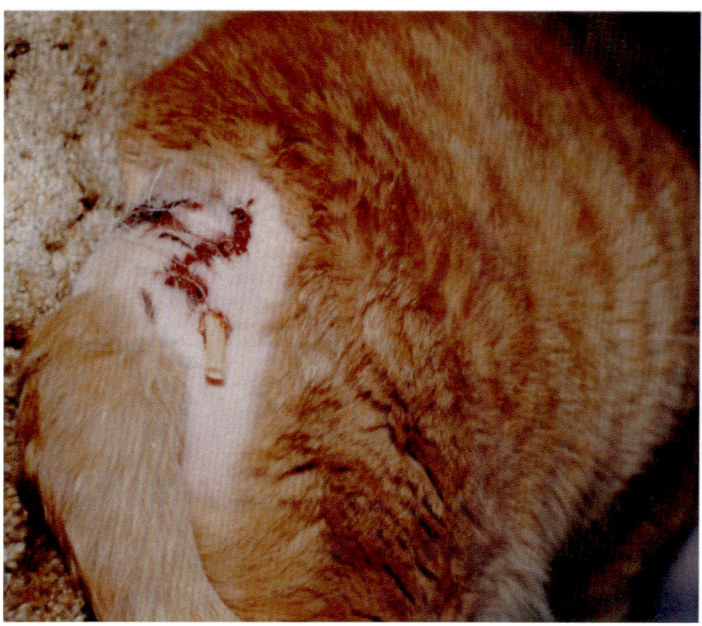

Tiger –
Recuperating after yet another Surgery

THE VET'S OFFER TO KEEP TIGER AT HIS CLINIC

Three months before we moved to Shuswap Lake, Tiger was due for his annual vaccinations and wellness checkup.

Dr. Thomas was very fond of Tiger, and he tended to all of Tiger's primary medical care during the 14 years of Tiger's very active life – from when he was brought into the clinic for the first time as a 6-day-old orphan kitten.

The veterinarian had performed surgery on Tiger after a traumatic ride in the motor of a pickup, and again after he was viciously attacked and carried away by a silver fox.

Tiger's life has not been like that of an ordinary cat. His life was a challenge from birth onward, and he has overcome many obstacles – which has made him strong and fearless.

Just before we left the patients' room to say a "forever goodbye," the doctor closed the door again and said: "We would love to keep Tiger at our clinic permanently." He could actually sit on the receptionist counter as a greeter! Of course, he would be free to roam certain areas." He also pointed out that it would leave Dennis and myself free to travel.

Nothing made sense to me. I asked him what else Tiger would be doing? He reluctantly admitted that my cat would be a perfect blood donor. It set me back a bit!!

In fact, Tiger had been used twice as a blood donor for two emergency surgeries. I knew that he met all required criteria; he was healthy and he was up-to-date with his vaccinations.

The vet's suggestion meant that my awesome furry child would donate lifesaving blood and plasma for felines in need. As with people, sick and injured dogs or cats sometimes require blood transfusions. It takes less than 30 minutes for a cat or dog to donate blood; it generally does not require any sedation; and as the owner, you can stay with your pet during the procedure. Blood is typically collected six times a year, but a pet can donate every three weeks if an emergency arises.

This offer by the vet was in the fall of 1991, when blood donation for cats and dogs was still simple. Today, the requirements for being eligible blood donor are stricter. The cat must be a certain weight and age, and it must take regular medication for the preventing of flea bites, ticks and heart worm.

A cat's blood is different than a dog's blood. Cats have a blood group system the AB system, which consists of three blood types – A, B and AB.

Surprisingly, my cat, who was always a terror in the car, was now sound asleep in his little dog carrier.

My mind was wandering: How would life be without my furry being? How would Dennis react to the vet's generous offer?

I settled Tiger with his evening feeding. Then I prepared our supper – easy cooking, as it was – leftovers from our previous evening meal. Afterwards we relaxed in the living room...now was the time to bring up this delicate subject and discuss what the doctor had suggested.

The unforgiving look on Dennis' face was like I had just stabbed him with a knife. He could not believe what I was saying.

After he had collected himself, he asked me: if I really meant what I was suggesting... "Really, are you out of your mind? That would be like giving away our four-legged furry son, and for what? Deserting your beloved cat you so much cared for! You attended to all his medical needs during fourteen years of his life...no, I don't want to hear about it again!

A guilty feeling came over me, and I felt foolish, ashamed for having spoken so cruelly. How could I have been so harsh?

The following day, I phoned the veterinarian and explained my husband's decision that we would, never part with Tiger.

This was an easy decision, and on February 26th, 1992 was moving day for Dennis and me, and for Mila and Tiger.

MOVING TO THE LAKE

The move to Shuswap Lake was a big undertaking, as it was an eight-hour car ride for Tiger in his kennel. The pick-up was loaded with potted plants and breakable items packed in boxes.

Tiger's kennel was again situated in the back seat on top of several boxes. Two hours before leaving town, I drove with Tiger to the vet clinic. Dr. Thomas advised me to sedate Tiger for the trip, so it would be less stress on my cat and on myself. To my surprise, our feline was very calm during our visit at the vet clinic; he did not even flinch when given the injection.

Saying goodbye to Dr. Thomas and his staff was very emotional. They had treated Tiger since he was eight days old, and for 14 years, Dr. Thomas had also treated our other pets.

For comfort, I had made a soft bed in Tiger's kennel - a layer of two folded towels, and on top a standard size, down-filled pillow with a pillow cover. Then I attached a water container, which was special made for the kennel and fit to the door. Tiger was asleep in no time.

There was no time to be wasted, and I started driving south. Winter road conditions in February were not exactly fun to drive. Mila sat on the front passenger seat, which was big enough for her to curl up and sleep. I took advantage of the quiet time and drove non-stop for almost four hours, until I had to stop to gas up the truck, and also to let Mila walk around for a bit. Then we had to continue our trip. When we entered the truck, Tiger was awake. He was calm as he greeted us with a meow, and I ignored him. It was dark, and I had to keep driving to my destination without any further stops.

Now that we had driven further south, the roads were in good condition and free of ice and snow. So, I was able to speed up. On the highway, Tiger again let out a kitten cry, which meant that he was in need of something. But he was still calm, and I kept driving.

Then, all of a sudden, I heard him scratching the bottom of the kennel, and I could hear him peeing.

And I noticed him re-arranging his bed. He then went back to sleep until we reached our new home.

First, I brought Tiger's litter box. I had left a little of his old sand in the box, to make him feel at home. Then I added new litter to fill the box.

Finally, Tiger was able to enter his new home. He immediately used his litter box and then cried for his meal. After he ate, he walked around the house, which was already setup for everything we needed, including our bed, and Tiger made himself right at home in our bedroom.

The next day, when we emptied the truck, I took the kennel aside to remove the bedding. Tiger had lifted the towels and had peed on the kennel floor. He then covered the floor with the towels, which sucked up the urine. So, the feather bed was totally dry for him to sleep on. Smart cat! I then disposed of everything, cleaned the kennel, and stored it away, hoping that we wouldn't have to use it again for a long time.

Tiger kept standing at the balcony sliding door, obviously wanting to go out, but my husband was afraid that Tiger might wander off. So, Dennis blocked off the gate of the balcony with a large tarp, thinking this would keep Tiger safely on the balcony, which was off the second floor of the house.

Then we let Tiger go unto the balcony, which overlooked the beach and the lake. He sat by the sliding door and watched his new surroundings, and I was pleased to see him so content. The sun by the sliding door was warm enough for me to leave the door ajar, and that way the cat could walk in and out at will.

A short time later, I checked on Tiger, but he was no longer on the balcony. We searched the house, but found no cat. Then I walked to the balcony gate and tried to remove the tarp, but it was heavy because Tiger was sitting on the outside of the gate on the tarp, it was leaning over the stairway. Most likely, Tiger had jumped unto the balcony railing and balanced along until he reached the gate and then jumped.

He showed us that it was okay for him to be outside of his new home. He was very timid and stayed close to us, and he actually loved that it was February and he could enjoy the outdoors during the day. And I could keep a watchful eye on him. He now was a content senior cat.

LIVING AT THE LAKE

In Tiger's life, we moved twice, and the last move – to Shuswap Lake – turned him into a completely different character. He actually became a timid cat. But clearly loved his new life, and Mila the dog became his forever companion.

It only took Tiger a few days to explore his new surroundings. There was water and a lot of it – a large lake. There was an old broken dock floating near the beach. A new safer dock was built shortly after. This new dock had been anchored with a chain bolted into a cement block in the water – to keep the dock permanently in place.

Step-by-step, Tiger ventured onto the dock. Because the water level of the lake was always very low in spring, the dock was partly grounded on the beach. In the beginning of June, with warmer temperatures and the snow melting in the mountains, the water level in the lake would rise rapidly, and the entire dock would float on the lake, but it was still secured.

Mila, our English Springer Spaniel, was a water dog, and she would jump off any dock into a lake or river, regardless of the extremely cold water temperature. However, at some point, old age prevented her from continuing this fun pastime. She was just not as mobile and agile as she used to be – so instead, she would slowly stroll into the lake for a short swim.

Eventually, Tiger would join Mila in the lake for a short dip to cool off. After, they would both lie on the dock or on the balcony, grooming themselves and relaxing in the sun.

Tiger – A Cool Swim in the Lake.

CHOOSING HIS FAVORITE PEOPLE

In general Tiger tolerated our grand-children, mostly if they were visiting more often during the year. Little Emily, clearly had been Tiger's favorite, she would lay beside him, whenever he was lying on the bed. She then would cover both of them under a blanket and then cuddle up to Tiger, while he was purring to let her know that he was happy.

Then during the summer Julie would come to visit us at the lake, with her parents and her two older sisters. Her sisters showed no interest in Tiger, and he in return ignored the two girls completely.

However, six year old Julie loved Mila, and of course our dog was everybody's friend. So Julie thought it should be the same way with Tiger. But Tiger was no friend of Julie. As harder she tried, as more annoyed he became with her.

One day I watched Julie trying to convince my cat, as he was lying on the master-bedroom bed. His eyes wide open and starring at Julie. His front paws stretched out and his ear lying flat to the back, which meant in Tiger's attitude; "Do not mess with me."

Julie, ever so careful approached Tiger, but the cat hissed at her. Frustrated Julie didn't leave the room, but begged Tiger; "But Tiger, you don't understand that I love you and I want to be your friend, don't you get it, all I want is for you to like me." But Tiger never budged and he never became close to the girls. I felt sorry for poor Julie, she tried her darnedest to please Tiger, but failed.

It was much different when my mom came visiting from Germany ones a year for a few months. Tiger followed her step by step, meowing up to her, until she picked him up and carried him around in her arms. While she was visiting, Tiger slept with her most nights.

Then when my mother flew back home, Tiger would be sadly looking for her and he slept on her pillow for many days and nights.

THE LIFE OF FERAL CATS

Another term for feral is 'free-roaming the streets'
As I mentioned before, we frequently observed feral cats or coyotes in the 10-acre field adjacent to a gravel road and to our house.

Feral cats are mostly not-owned or escaped domestic cats that live outdoors to avoid human contact. The cat does not allow anyone to catch them or handle them, and they typically remain hidden from humans.

Feral cats breed over dozens of generations and they can become very aggressive in urban environments. They are mostly active after dusk.

Feral are devastating to wildlife, and one of the worst species on earth. Most feral live in outdoors colonies.

Some animal-rights group advocate trap-neuter-return-programs to prevent the cats from continuing to breed, and they advocate for feeding the cat. If socialized, the young feral cats and kittens have a chance of being adopted, where they will be provided with regular food, and a loving and safe environment, with good health care.

Definitions of feral and stray cats: The meaning of the term 'feral cat' varies between countries. They are often called 'alley cats' or 'community cats'. Some of these terms are also used to refer to stray cats, but stray and feral cats are considered to be very different.

The idea is that house cats that wander away from their homes may become stray cats that live in the wild for some time, and then may become feral cats. Then they can eventually choose not to interact with human.

Some domestic cats that have been abandoned or gotten lost can then turn feral in order to survive.

TIGER'S ENCOUNTER
WITH FERAL CATS

By June 1993, we had settled into our new home and our surroundings quite nicely, and most of the necessary renovations had been completed.

The garden we had planted was already producing a variety of vegetables, as well as raspberries, and we had also planted fruit trees. Our families and friends who visited us during the Summer and Fall always enjoyed the bounty of our garden.

Longer days and warm weather enticed Tiger to venture further away from our property. Often, he did not return until late at night when I called him to come home. He liked to roam the field looking for gophers – the furry rodents that were all around our neighbor's properties.

In fact, there are about 35 different species of gophers that are endemic to Northern/Central America and Canada. They are called Northern Pocket Gophers, or just Gophers, and they are brown in color and grow about 18 cm long, (not included their long bushy tail). Gophers are commonly known for their extensive tunneling activities that can destroy farms and gardens, and they live underground in these burrows. Then in the winter, they hibernate for nine months.

I quite often observed coyotes and feral cats hunting in the field for gophers. Apparently, gophers made for a good meal.

Our master bedroom window looked over our lawn and towards a gravel road and the adjacent well fenced field.

Early in the morning, while making the bed, I was keeping watch for Tiger, who had not returned from the previous night. I kept calling him, hoping that he would come home safely, but there was no sign of my beloved cat

Then I saw Tiger far out in the field, and I could see that he was limping on three legs and dragging his right front leg.

I rushed to meet him, and I saw that he had been severely injured. Overall, it appeared that he might have been hit by a car. My poor beloved Tiger was muddy, wet and bloody. My first thought was that perhaps he had been thrown into a ditch – lying there in pain, or maybe for a short time unconscious before gaining his strength and courage to crawl home on three legs.

As I lifted him up, he hissed at me, which was very unusual. He was letting me know that he was suffering and that I had to be gentle. Our tough Tabby was in severe agony.

Dennis and I immediately drove our cat 68 km to the Salmon Arm vet clinic. The doctor sedated Tiger so he could stabilize him for dehydration and pain control. Once Tiger settled, his wounded leg was x-rayed, and it did not appear to be broken. We were relieved about that.

However, his elbow and leg were severely swollen, and the next procedure was for his leg to be totally shaved. The veterinarian pointed out that Tiger had numerous puncture wounds with red round lesions that were very tender and painful.

The vet concluded that Tiger must have encountered several feral cats and he obviously could not win that fight. Feral cat scratches and bite wounds carry disease and bacterial infection, and they can transmit rabies and tetanus.

It appeared that Tiger's leg had swollen to twice the size and was already infected. He also had a dangerously high fever.

Our beloved cat was admitted into the animal hospital. He needed an IV catheter for antibiotics, as well as for fluid, and he required further observation to check for other vital signs.

Meanwhile, my husband and I were booked for a two-week vacation, and we were supposed to be leaving in a few days. The kind veterinarian offered to keep and care for Tiger in the clinic while we were away.

After our return from the most beautiful, relaxed holiday, we eagerly drove to the vet-clinic to claim our greater-than-life cat.

Tiger's injuries had almost healed, and he was released to go home. Before we left, the doctor remarked: "It is funny that Tiger tends to walk without a limp if nobody is watching; but if you look directly at him, or ask him "How is Tiger"? without fail, he will start to limp again – but only for a short time.

If we showed him a treat, he would forget to limp. For him, food was the most important thing in life.

Tiger completely avoided the field after that incident, he preferred relaxing on our dock, which was floating off the beach in front of our house.

However, this was not without danger either, because during the winter and early spring, the Bald Eagles would quite often fly above Shuswap Lake and the surrounding area in search of food. Several times, when Tiger walked by himself onto the dock or along the beach, a Bald Eagle would spot my cat from the air. Luckily, I could see this from the window facing our beach. I would run like a mad woman, screaming up into the air, and then snatch Tiger and rush him into the house.

Hid did not know how close he had come, several times, to being an Eagles feast.

OUR DIABETIC CAT

In February 1994, Dennis and I decided to tour Vancouver Island with our dog Mila and visit our friends and relatives. As always, our senior friend Arnold stayed at our house. He lived down the road from us, and during the winter, he was the security guard for several houses, lake cabins, and neighbors' properties and one farm, to prevent break-ins and vandalism, while owners were away.

Tiger adored Arnold, and he enjoyed cuddling up to him while watching TV. As noted, our feline was indoors only during the winter. In summer, Tiger often walked to the end of the 10-acre field to visit Arnold at his little house. Then he would lay for hours in the sun on Arnold's sundeck.

Usually, Tiger greeted us at the inside of the front door whenever we returned home. But that evening, our cat was nowhere to be seen. We called his name, but there was no reply. Searching throughout the house, we discovered him sitting under the faucet in the bathtub, frantically banging his front paws against the spout and trying to get a sip of water. It puzzled us, because his drinking bowl was empty.

I phoned Arnold, and he told me that he had filled the water bowl in the morning when he fed Tiger. Arnold was in town that day, knowing that we would be home later.

My husband realized that our beloved cat was diabetic and that he was severely dehydrated. I filled the water bowl immediately, and it was empty in no time.

On Monday morning, I phoned the vet clinic so Tiger could be seen as soon as possible.

---"What for?" asked the receptionist.

---"Because Tiger is diabetic."

---"Says who?" She laughed and said, "Just bring him in on Wednesday at 2:30 p.m.

In my frustration, I hung up the phone, put Tiger in his kennel, and drove the 68 km to the vet clinic in Salmon Arm.

There was a new receptionist, and I told her that this was my diabetic cat. Two other assistants noticed me and Tiger, and they were happy to see Tiger again., and within 5 minutes, he was examined by a vet.

His urine and blood tests proved Dennis' suspicion to be right, and Tiger was kept overnight for further observation.

The following day, my husband and I met with the veterinarian to be counseled regarding Tiger's condition and treatments. Tiger would need insulin injections twice a day at feeding time, and apparently the exact timing was everything. We were supplied with a 20 ml bottle of insulin and small, sharp injection needles.

The starting dose of 0,25 units had to be administered twice daily. Tiger's weight at that time was

24 pounds, which was considered to be a very large cat. The insulin used for humans was also used for treating cats in those days. Eventually he was given doses of 0.8 units, exactly at each feeding.

Tiger was a great patient, and he never complained when a needle was inserted into his shoulder, where the skin was loose and easy to inject. He realized that an injection came with being fed. If he got hungry, he would sit in front of the kitchen cupboard where his food was being kept and for his regular treatment and meal.

In those days, I would pour boiling water with a drop of hydrogen peroxide 3% USP over the syringes and let them soak for 15 minutes. Then I would lay them on a fresh, clean tea towel to dry. Discarding syringes was unheard of.

Dennis always performed the blood test for the highest and lowest glucose reading for the day, and the blood sugar test six hours after feeding. This required us to regular prick our pet's paw, or else just behind the ear, but our feline took it all in stride.

If I could not find Tiger, all I needed to do was press the electric can opener and he would fly into the kitchen, knowing that food was being prepared.

Once a month, Tiger had to visit the vet clinic. He was always stressed out when it came to a car ride, which was a nightmare for Tiger and nerve-wrecking for us.

In conjunction with the insulin, another key element of treatment was his diet modification. The cat was overweight, particularly during the winter when he tended to be less active and to sleep more. Not to mention that by now he was a senior cat. So it was a must to gradually introduce a weight loss diet for him, high in fiber and low in calories. The vet clinic sold specially prepared canned diet food that proved to be very beneficial. After three months, Tiger's weight was roughly 21 pounds, which was perfect for his size.

Spring arrived and our cat was outdoors during the days again. He spent a lot of time on the dock with his canine buddy Mila. Or the two senior pets would lie for hours on the sundeck enjoying the warmth of spring. They no longer played with the grandchildren, or with toys. Instead they just enjoyed each other's company.

Summer and Fall came and went, and Tiger was very fit and continued to improve. My husband only periodically checked Tiger's blood/glucose. He had a discussion with our vet and it was decided to lower the insulin every seven days. Every change was observed, like keeping a dairy.

Nineteen months from day one of being diagnosed a diabetic, Tiger no longer needed insulin. What a relief for all of us! As for his special diet, he was kept on it for the rest of his life.

My husband, who once said, he did not want to keep the adorable and needy eight-days-old kitten, is now always attentive to his needs and his wellbeing.

SAYING GOOD-BYE

The hardest part of loving a pet is saying good-bye. But we do find comfort in our happy memories of the time spent with our furry, loving friends and our family members.

Dear as my two pets were, I had to learn to cope with losing them both, and then to cope with the situation of being alone again.

Tiger suffered severely with kidney failure and had to be humanely euthanized. He fell asleep peacefully in my arms. It was two months before his 20th birthday.

Mila died of a massive stroke at the age of fourteen. She was an extremely smart and very obedient dog.

My two pets passed away six weeks apart in the summer of 1998 and both were cremated.

They were forever faithful....

and then forever at peace.